SAMURAI
STRATEGIES

SAMURAI STRATEGIES

42 Martial Secrets from Musashi's *Book of Five Rings*

BOYÉ LAFAYETTE DE MENTE

TUTTLE Publishing

Tokyo | Rutland, Vermont | Singapore

The Tuttle Story: "Books to Span the East and West"

Most people are surprised to learn that the world's leading publisher of books on Asia had humble beginnings in the tiny American state of Vermont. The company's founder, Charles E. Tuttle, belonged to a New England family steeped in publishing. And his fi rst love was naturally books—especially old and rare editions.

Immediately after WWII, serving in Tokyo under General Douglas MacArthur, Tuttle was tasked with reviving the Japanese publishing industry. He later founded the Charles E. Tuttle Publishing Company, which thrives today as one of the world's leading independent publishers.

Though a westerner, Tuttle was hugely instrumental in bringing a knowledge of Japan and Asia to a world hungry for information about the East. By the time of his death in 1993, Tuttle had published over 6,000 books on Asian culture, history and art—a legacy honored by the Japanese emperor with the "Order of the Sacred Treasure," the highest tribute Japan can bestow upon a non-Japanese.

With a backlist of 1,500 titles, Tuttle Publishing is more active today than at any time in its past—still inspired by Charles Tuttle's core mission to publish fi ne books to span the East and West and provide a greater understanding of each.

ACKNOWLEDGMENT

I am indebted to my publisher Eric Oey for suggesting this book, and to my editor Ed Walters for making the text far more readable and useful to anyone wanting to achieve success in today's world.

Published by Tuttle Publishing, an imprint of Periplus Editions (HK) Ltd.

www.tuttlepublishing.com

Copyright © 2008 Boyé Lafayette De Mente

Library of Congress Control Number: 2008925549

ISBN 978-0-8048-3950-1

First edition
18 17 16 15   10 9 8 7 6 5 4
1505CM

Distributed by

North America, Latin America & Europe
Tuttle Publishing
364 Innovation Drive, North Clarendon,
VT 05759-9436 U.S.A.
Tel: 1 (802) 773-8930; Fax: 1 (802) 773-6993
info@tuttlepublishing.com
www.tuttlepublishing.com

Japan
Tuttle Publishing
Yaekari Building, 3rd Floor, 5-4-12 Osaki,
Shinagawa-ku, Tokyo 141 0032
Tel: (81) 3 5437-0171; Fax: (81) 3 5437-0755
sales@tuttle.co.jp
www.tuttle.co.jp

Asia Pacific
Berkeley Books Pte. Ltd.
61 Tai Seng Avenue #02-12, Singapore 534167
Tel: (65) 6280-1330; Fax: (65) 6280-6290
inquiries@periplus.com.sg
www.periplus.com

Printed in China

TUTTLE PUBLISHING® is a registered trademark of Tuttle Publishing, a division of Periplus Editions (HK) Ltd.

Contents

PREFACE

The Seven Virtues of the Samurai Way

Many societies have had classes or groups of people who were extraordinary in ways that made them famous or notorious or both. One of the largest and most famous of these classes of people were the samurai of feudal Japan—the hereditary professional warrior class that ruled the country from 1192 until 1868, during which time they made up from ten to twelve percent of the population.

The defining characteristics of the samurai culture were based on a number of Shinto, Buddhist, Confucian, and Zen concepts that were to make it unique and provide it with the power to dramatically change the history of Japan, and over the course of time to have a fundamental impact on the rest of the world.

One of the most important elements in the samurai culture was the concept of the fragility and briefness of life. Members of the samurai class were taught from childhood that life is as fragile as a cherry blossom that can be wafted away by the slightest breeze, and that they should live their lives accordingly, obeying all of the obligations that made up their world so that they could die at any moment without remorse for having failed to live up to their responsibilities.

Samurai warriors generally followed this philosophy of life with profound diligence for two very simple reasons. First, they were, in fact, subject to being killed, or having to kill themselves and sometimes their families as well, at a moment's notice. And second, they firmly believed that if they failed to behave according to the precepts that controlled their class they and their families would be shamed and disgraced forever.

The samurai understood that if people were acutely aware that they could die at a moment's notice they would be far more likely to embrace what became known as the *Shichi Toku* (She-chee Toh-kuu), or "The Seven Virtues," that were to become the foundation of their culture.

These seven virtues, which were taught as the moral and ethical guidelines of the samurai, became the code of conduct prescribed for them (their "Commandments" if you will). The virtues covered virtually all of the areas and topics of human interest and needs, especially those that involved appearance, personal relationships, and living life according to a strict etiquette that was prescribed down to the smallest detail.

Over the centuries of the samurai rule, these same virtues gradually became an integral part of the culture of the common people as well. And they were to play a fundamental role in the transformation of Japan from an agrarian society to an industrialized nation between 1870 and 1890, in the recovery of Japan after the devastation of World War II, and in the astounding emergence of Japan as the world's second largest economy in less than 30 years after the end of the war.

The First Virtue of the Samurai

The first of the seven virtues that became the foundation of the education of the samurai is expressed in the term *kennin* (kane-neen), which can be translated as indomitable spirit, fortitude and perseverance. From childhood, both boys and girls in the samurai class were taught and required to demonstrate the attributes of *kennin* in all of the facets of their lives.

Their training literally began in infancy, with babies still in arms being instructed in when and how to bow properly, followed by constant instruction in all of the basic elements of a very precise etiquette that included how to dress, how to eat, how to sit, how to bathe, how and when to use respect language, to withstand cold without complaining, to withstand pain without flinching, to never give up on anything they set out to do, to revenge any insult, and to immediately obey the orders of superiors—including orders to commit suicide.

Training of samurai youth included the physical, emotional, intellectual, and spiritual elements of the body and mind, and was centered on the martial arts.

From around the age of six or seven all samurai boys who were not physically or mentally impaired were required to engage in training in *kendō* (kendohh), literally "the way of the sword" and figuratively fighting with a sword—first using wooden swords or wooden staffs in their training sessions.

This training, overseen by instructors, generally took place every day for several hours, becoming more intense as the boys approached their teen years. Youths were formally and officially recognized as "samurai warriors" when they became fifteen years old, at which time they were required to wear two swords at all times when they were in public—a long sword for attacking others or defending themselves, and a short sword for committing suicide when that occasion arose.

Young samurai who were assigned to military units of the shogunate and fief lords were required to continue their regular training until they were killed or retired from wounds or old age. Those who became administrators, including the highest ministers and the shoguns themselves, also continued regular training in *kendō* throughout their active lives.

All shoguns, vice-shoguns, fief lords, and ranking members of the shogunate and fiefdoms had their own *kendō* training centers staffed by masters. In addition to their own personal training, they regularly sponsored exhibition bouts and tournaments to increase the knowledge and skills of their warriors.

The masters in these training centers were invariably middle-aged and older warriors who had gained fame by killing many opponents during their earlier careers, and in numerous cases had developed their own style of sword-fighting that they taught in their "schools."

The training in *kendō* and other martial arts was taken very seriously by the samurai class because of the competition and intrigue that was typical among the fiefs of feudal Japan, and fear among shoguns that one or more of the fief lords would rebel against them.

One example of the lengths to which some samurai fathers went in training their sons in *kendō* was the practice of having them cut the heads off of several convicts or prisoners to get the feel of it and to be able to do it efficiently.

In one famous historical example of this kind of practice, some ten condemned men were lined up in a

row and a fifteen-year-old samurai youth was instructed to decapitate all of them one after the other. He rap-
idly cut the heads off of all of the men except one
before stopping and saying that he was tired and would
spare the man's life.

This was the kind and degree of *kennin* that was
expected and demanded of the samurai, and is one of
the facets of the samurai legacy that still today is very
much in evidence in the character and behavior of
many Japanese.

The Second Virtue of the Samurai

The second virtue that was a key part of the world of
the samurai was *shinnen* (sheen-nane), which refers to
conviction and faith. The demanding life of the samurai required that they develop extraordinary conviction
in their beliefs and behavior. It also required that they
have absolute faith in their ability to succeed in life
despite its challenges.

Over the generations these *shinnen* traits became so
deeply embedded in the character and personality of
the samurai that they developed a complex that led
most of them to believe that they could do anything
they set out to do.

This complex was to have a powerful influence on
Japan as a whole—aesthetically, economically, politi-
cally, and militarily. In some cases this influence was

positive; in other cases it was negative.

Some of the results of the negative side of this complex became well-known internationally in the 19th and 20th centuries because of military campaigns by the Japanese against Korea, Russia, China, Southeast Asian countries, and the U.S.

On the positive side, the superiority complex of the Japanese, buttressed by unbounded *shinnen*, contributed enormously to their success in turning their war-devastated country into the world's second largest economy in one short generation.

While the present-day cultural and technological accomplishments of the Japanese have not been officially attributed to the superiority complex of the samurai, they nevertheless are manifestations of the conviction and faith—and pride—that the Japanese have in their ability to create, innovate, and accomplish things...and, in fact, are an extension of the traditional built-in belief that they are—or were—a superior people because of their samurai heritage.

Still today there are influential people in Japan who continue to maintain that Japan's samurai-derived culture is superior to all others, and to claim that only the principles and practices of the samurai can save the world from the weaknesses of market capitalism, democracy, and individual freedom.

The Third Samurai Virtue

The third paramount virtue that Japan's samurai had to develop from a very early age was that of exercising extreme *shincho* (sheen-choh), meaning care, caution, and discretion, in their daily lives.

Even when very young it was necessary for the samurai to be extraordinarily careful in the way they behaved toward others because of the demands of their formalized, ritualized and unforgiving etiquette. As they grew older, these demands became even stronger and more encompassing.

There were occasions when something as simple as a failure to bow in the established and expected manner could mean death—sometimes instantly. Giving the "wrong" gift or no gift at all to a high-ranking person could be equally disastrous—making it imperative that they know the rules and follow the details of those rules precisely. (There were as many as 400 precise rules for giving a gift to certain people.)

In addition to following the guidelines of printed etiquette manuals, the samurai developed a cultural sixth sense that helped guide them through the intricacies of their system of behavior—first because it was a matter of survival, and as time passed because it became a matter of both honor and pride.

Most present-day Japanese, particularly the older generations, have retained much of the traditional built-in *shincho* reaction in their relationships with others because the level of day-to-day physical and verbal etiquette remains high by world standards.

The caution factor in Japanese behavior invariably kicks into high gear when they are dealing with non-Japanese. It is therefore especially important for foreigners dealing with Japanese to be aware of this factor in their character in order to accurately evaluate their actions and reactions.

The *tatemae* (tah-tay-my), or "façade" element in Japanese speech (that I explore in detail in my book, *Japan's Cultural Code Words* (Tuttle Publishing), is an extension of the *shincho* factor.

The built-in *shincho* compass of the Japanese typically results in them concealing their *honne* (hoan-nay), their true thoughts and intensions, at the beginning of negotiations with a ritualistic facade that is only gradually removed as the dialogue progresses…if the opposing side is aware enough of what is going on and persists in chipping away at it.

The Fourth Samurai Virtue

Despite the often ruthless and barbaric aspect of the culture of the samurai there was an underlying theme of *seigi* (say-ee-ghee), or righteousness and justice, in their moral and ethical code.

Japan's feudal history is, in fact, filled with examples of the extraordinary sense of righteousness and justice of typical samurai leaders as well as lower ranked members of the class. These examples included such things as demonstrations of goodwill and honesty that were above and beyond what was normal then and now.

In fact, the level of goodwill and honesty has been exceptionally high among virtually all Japanese since ancient times because of the influence of Confucianism, but it was made even more so by the code of the samurai.

I recall a number of such instances in my own early years in Japan in the 1940s and 50s. On one occasion I stayed overnight at a small inn in the Akabane district of Tokyo, and forgot a raincoat there when I left the next morning.

Some two years later, during which time I totally forgot about the coat, I went back to the inn. The instant I stepped into the entrance foyer the proprietress of the inn said: "Ah! Mr. De Mente! You forgot your raincoat!" She then took it out of a wooden box behind the counter and handed it to me, neatly folded.

Many of the historical examples of the manifestations of *seigi* are far more telling. Among these are common occasions when retainers of fief lords or other high-ranking samurai would become disillusioned with the morality and ethics of their superiors and commit suicide, leaving a message beseeching them to mend their ways; a very powerful way of getting their point across.

I remember at the end of World War II some American businesspeople were amazed when Japanese companies informed them that they would honor prewar debts and other obligations owed to the Americans, even when the American firms no longer had records of such debts.

In present-day Japan examples of *seigi* range from ordinary people going to extremes to return lost items to their rightful owners—including wallets containing money—to businesspeople who remain loyal to partners and suppliers even when it is seriously disadvantageous for them to do so.

The Fifth Virtue of the Samurai

Another element in the character of the samurai that recent history might seem to discount was the importance and role of *sessei* (say-ssay-ee), or moderation and temperance. From their youth the samurai were indoctrinated in the Buddhist and Confucian concepts of moderation and temperance.

The strictness of the samurai culture in enforcing *sessei* in their own class resulted in the majority of them being extraordinarily self-restrained in their behavior, not only to uphold the honor of their family and class but also as a matter of survival, since they were extraordinarily sensitive to slights or insults brought on by intemperance or ill will and were obligated to avenge against such incidents by killing the individual concerned.

The common people of Japan were under even more pressure to behave in the prescribed manner and avoid intemperance of any kind, especially in their dealings with samurai because the penalty for displeasing a samurai could be fatal.

In fact, during the early years of the last shogunate dynasty (the Tokugawa Shogunate, 1603-1868), it was made the law of the land that a samurai could kill on the spot any commoner who failed to show him the prescribed respect. The samurai could then apologize and walk away. This law was known as *kirisute gomen* (kee-ree-suu-tay go-mane), literally "regretful killing." [*Kirisute* means to cut down, the common Japanese word for kill during the samurai era, and *gomen* means "sorry."]

Obviously, all this is not to say that most samurai themselves were paragons of *sessei*, but the majority did scrupulously abide by the etiquette prescribe for their class, resulting in a level of temperance that was extraordinarily high by world standards.

The *sessei*-bound samurai not only served as role models for the common people of Japan, they set the standards of behavior that commoners were expected to follow, and enforced these standards with strict, immediate measures that made ordinary Japanese among the best behaved people on the planet.

The heritage of *sessei* remains visible in present-day Japan. The standard of public behavior is exceptionally high despite inroads made by foreign cultures and a general relaxation of the strict rules of etiquette that were followed and enforced by the samurai—and despite the fact that Japan has one of the world's largest night-time entertainment industries and that nightly huge numbers of people are out on the town having a good and often boisterous time

This latter interesting incongruity is a result of the fact that there is a strict division between the formal, stylized behavior of the Japanese during the day when *sessei* prevails, and their after-hours behavior, particularly in drinking situations when it is formally recognized that you can dispense with the strict etiquette that is a legacy of the samurai era.

The Sixth Samurai Virtue

Jizen (jee-zane), or benevolence and charity, was the sixth virtue that samurai were expected to follow, and most did with extraordinary diligence during the long samurai era, leaving a legacy that is still a part of the character of the average Japanese.

It may be difficult for people who are only casually

acquainted with the history of the samurai to associate benevolence and charity with samurai warriors during the long feudal era—as well as after the samurai system was abolished in 1870 and the sword-carrying warriors were recast in the mode of Western-style military forces of the day.

By contemporary Western standards much of the behavior of the samurai during both the pre-and-post samurai periods was, in fact, barbaric and savage. But, historically, it was not that different from the practices that existed in the West during the Middle-Ages, and which did not begin to change until the latter part of the 1800s...the same period when the samurai class was dissolved.

But behind the public image of the samurai as barbaric and brutal, the Buddhist concept of benevolence and charity was followed most of the time by most samurai, including those in positions of authority. There are many historical examples of city and town samurai magistrates who were famous for their wisdom and benevolence.

The same *jizen* traits of benevolence and charity that were an important part of the training of samurai had, in fact, been characteristic of ordinary Japanese throughout their history as a result of the influence of Shinto and Buddhism, and continue to this day.

One of my favorite anecdotes that emphasizes the

character and behavior of the typical Japanese shortly after the end of the samurai era involves the famous writer-author Lafcadio Hearn. He went to Japan in the 1890s on an assignment for an American magazine and was so entranced by the behavior of the Japanese he proclaimed that living in Japan was like living in paradise, and remained there for the rest of his life.

Hearn was referring to the refined etiquette, the innate hospitality, and the incredible honesty and goodwill of ordinary Japanese. This cultural factor remains very much in evidence today and is one of the reasons why most present-day foreigners in Japan find living there so seductive, as Hearn did more than a hundred years ago.

The Seventh Samurai Virtue

Kibō (kee-bohh), or hope, is another virtue that one might have difficulty associating with Japan's samurai class and their militaristic descendants in more recent times.

But despite the many cultural and governmental restraints that limited the options and opportunities of the Japanese prior to modern times, the Japanese were not a morose or morbid people. They had a marvelous sense of humor, loved jokes and puns, and since ancient times have had a variety of celebrations and parties of one kind or another throughout the year.

For one thing, the Japanese were also among the first people to travel widely—and safely—within their own country for recreational purposes, especially to enjoy the incredible beauty of both the mountain and coastal areas of the islands, and to visit famous shrines and temples scattered throughout the country.

And Japan was also the first country to have a nationwide network of roadside inns at regular shogunate-prescribed distances from each other that were specifically designed and managed to cater to travelers, virtually all of whom traveled on foot (also by government decree), and were therefore on the road for weeks at a time when traversing long distances.

All of these feel-good and enjoy-yourself aspects of Japanese culture were manifestations of the fact that the major religions of Japan—Shinto and Buddhism—were primarily based on positive and happy beliefs that included sensual pleasures of all kinds.

As the generations passed, *Kibō* and the six other virtues promoted by the samurai gradually impregnated the mindset of all Japanese, and continue to this day to distinguish them from other people.

Again, this is not to infer that all of Japan's samurai were paragons of these primary virtues, or to ignore the fact that the definitions and nuances of all of these virtues were based on Japanese values and aspirations, which often differed fundamentally from Western precepts.

But within Japanese society during the age of the samurai the level of ethics, manners, morality and overall behavior was as high—if not higher—than has ever been achieved before or since in any other society. And this encompassed many of the most desirable and admirable beliefs and behavioral traits that were part of the Hebrew and Christian traditions.

The overall legacy of the samurai remains today the foundation of Japan's etiquette, ethics and morality—significantly weakened by the importation of democratic ideals of individualism and selfishness from the West, primarily the United States, but nevertheless visible in every area of society.

Why Japan Became an Economic Superpower

It was, in fact, the legacy of the virtues of the samurai that made it possible for Japan to become the world's second largest economy between 1950 and 1975—notwithstanding the contributions derived from the wide-open American and European markets and the billions of dollars the United States government spent in Japan procuring supplies for the Korean and Vietnam wars.

Without the spirit, the perseverance, the will and the pride that had become the hallmarks of the samurai character, it is unlikely that the Japanese would have overcome the devastation and loss caused by their defeat in World War II, much less become an economic superpower in one short generation.

It therefore behooves the rest of the world to have more than a casual knowledge about the philosophy and character of the samurai class, especially that epitomized by the incredible Musashi Miyamoto.

And in a remarkable turn of events, this same need now applies to Japan itself because the social changes following the end of the 1941–1945 Pacific War (as the Japanese call it) resulted in the youth of Japan no longer being educated or trained in the positive virtues of the samurai.

There is now a great fear in Japan that the disappearance of the samurai spirit from the ethos of the Japanese, especially those born since the 1970s, is weakening the ability of the country to compete with the rest of the world, and will have even worse consequences in the future.

This fear has resulted in a rising tide of effort by social authorities, educators, government officials and business leaders to reintroduce the spirit of the samurai into the culture—and not all of these efforts are positive or desirable.

The most notorious—and so far best known—of these efforts is epitomized by mathematics professor Masahiko Fujiwara's book, *Kokka no Hinkaku* (Koke-kah no Heen-kah-kuu), or "The Dignity of a Nation."

In this book, which sold over two million copies during its first year on the market, he advocates a return to the dictatorial style of government and business management that existed in Japan prior to the introduction of democracy into the country following the end of World War II in 1945.

He, in fact, advocates the spread of Japan's samurai-type culture to the rest of the world in a manner that is reminiscent of the ideology that fueled Japan's militant aggression during the first half of the 20th century.

On the positive side of this movement is author and educator Michihiro Matsumoto who has patterned his life after that of Musashi Miyamoto, and whom I have labeled "The Most Dangerous Man in Japan" because of his lifelong commitment to asking why and forcing people to explain their opinions and policies—a very un-Japanese-like thing to do.

Matsumoto's book, *Nihon no Kigai* (Nee-hone no Kee-guy) or "The Spirit of a Nation"—written as a counterpoint to Professor Fujiwara's screed, is an appeal for the country to return to the shinto-based samurai virtues of the past that represent the intellectual and spiritual best of that remarkable class of people.

The most conspicuous evidence that Matsumoto's message about the importance of restoring the best elements of the samurai spirit and the need for the Japanese to learn how to debate—both of which he has been advocating since the 1980s—is gaining traction in the country is the growing number of martial arts studios that are attracting young men and women, and the expanding role of Zen mediation and the art of debating in business training.

Whatever the faults of the samurai culture—and there were many—it also contained extraordinary insights into human nature, and encouraged attitudes and behavior that represent the highest potential for humanity.

Musashi Miyamoto himself was an amazing product of the culture of the samurai, representing the extremes of its positive and negative elements. The positive elements in his classic treatise on fighting, *Go Rin Sho* (Go Reen Shoh), or "Book of Five Rings," contain fundamental wisdom that can be applied in constructive as well as destructive ways.

— *Boyé Lafayette De Mente*

The Most Dangerous Man in Japan!

This edition of *Samurai Strategies* includes commentary by Michihiro Matsumoto, an extraordinary individual whom I regard as the most dangerous man in Japan because he constantly bombards people with the question, "Why?" forcing them to explain their opinions, policies and actions.

Matsumoto is a martial artist, a simultaneous English-Japanese interpreter, scholar, professor, former NHK TV host, debate enthusiast, prolific author (over 100 books), and accomplished poet who is often referred to as Japan's "English Samurai" because of his use of samurai techniques in his study of English and in his overall approach to life. He not only vetted the manuscript prior to publication he graciously provided me with some comments to add to the book.

Matsumoto's appointment as a simultaneous inter-preter for the American Embassy in the early 1970s was especially noteworthy because he was the first (and as of this writing is still the only) person to pass the very rigorous simultaneous interpreter test without having studied outside of Japan. Furthermore, he learned English privately, on his own.

At the age of thirteen Matsumoto resolved to pat-tern his life after that of Japan's most famous samurai warrior, the iconoclastic Musashi Miyamoto (1584– 1645), author of the noted treatise *Go Rin Shō* (Go Reen Shoh), or *Book of Five Rings*, on which this book is based. Musashi himself was just thirteen years old when he began his astounding career as a duelist, killing a veteran warrior twice his age.

In addition to becoming a dedicated student of the martial arts as taught and practiced by Musashi, Matsumoto quickly realized that the principles that Musashi applied to the study and practice of *Kendō* (The Way of the Sword) could also be used in master-ing English. He subsequently devised his own method of study that he called *Eigodō*, or "The Way of English."

Matsumoto's decision to achieve perfection in Eng-lish by using his own *Eigodō* method meant that he ignored most of the institutionalized and ritualized behavior and knowledge of Japanese culture, resulting in him becoming known as a maverick—as someone who didn't think or act like a typical Japanese and who invariably upset the famous *wa* (wah), or harmony, that was the foundation of Japan's traditional culture.

Rather than follow the traditional way, Matsumoto's professional and public life became epitomized by his questioning of the characteristic Japanese way of thinking and acting. The word "why"—the term he constantly used in an effort to force people to publicly explain themselves and something that had long been taboo in Japanese society—became his trademark.

In the early 1980s he founded the Matsumoto Debate Institute, utilizing his revolutionary *Eigodō* method to teach people how to debate in both English and Japanese. His first book of note, written in 1984 in English, was the now classic *HARAGEI—Silence in Japanese Business and Society* (Kodansha International), which may be translated as "The Art of the Belly"—a seminal work that revealed for the first time the Japanese use of cultural knowledge and intuition in decision-making.

Haragei refers to the art of exuding energy, called *ki* (kee), from the *hara* (hah-rah)—the solar plexis in English terms—the large network of sympathetic nerves and ganglia located in the peritoneal cavity behind the stomach, and branching out from there.

Matsumoto defines *haragei* as the verbal and physi-

cal actions one employs to influence others by the
potency of rich experience and boldness, and dealing
with people and situations through ritual formalities.
He also defines it as "emotional communication"—
which aptly describes virtually all verbal and non-ver-
bal exchanges between the Japanese.

In 1986 Matsumoto became the president of the
Kodokan Debating Society and in 1998 he became
president of the International Debate Development
Association, concurrently serving as professor of Inter-
cultural Communications at Honolulu University.

Matsumoto's checkered career in commerce, government service, academia, and public broadcasting has
been about as un-Japanese-like as you can get because
in a culture in which employees didn't ask questions,
hunkered down, and remained with the same organization for life, he didn't stay quiet and he didn't assume a
low profile.

By the end of the 1990s Matsumoto's dedication to
the revolutionary why-because way of interacting with
other people had finally begun to pay off. A growing
number of Japanese had begun adopting his philosophy—a phenomenon that was to become particularly
conspicuous among some academics, senior business
executives, and leading politicians who had previously
been as quiet as mutes.

Matsumoto has, in fact, been something like a virus

that started out as a tiny irritant but has now begun to impact on Japan's contemporary culture in fundamental ways that are having a slow but profound affect on society in general.

This does not mean, however, that Matsumoto himself is no longer Japanese in any traditional sense. He is, in fact, more traditional in his overall philosophy than most of his contemporaries, having remained a strong advocate of the value of the fabled spirit of the samurai, and using this spirit as the foundation for his teaching.

In 2007 Matsumoto published *Nihon no Kigai* (Nee-hone no Kee-guy), or *The Spirit of Japan* [Nisshin Hodo], a call for Japan to return to the positive elements of the samurai way. I believe his philosophy represents not only the best path for Japan to follow in the future, but that it is also the country's best defense against those who advocate a return to the aggressive, militaristic principles and policies of the past.

And it is for these reasons that I am delighted to have commentary provided by Matsumoto in this book. We have been close friends and colleagues ever since the 1980s, and have collaborated on a number of books in both English and Japanese.

When I first announced my intention of distilling, in plain English, the essence of Miyamoto's famous but esoteric treatise on engaging in death duels with a sword, Matsumoto not only encouraged me to undertake the task, but he also volunteered to evaluate my version of the lessons Musashi taught, as well as add some commentary of his own to my explanations.

CHAPTER ONE

Set Goals

The goal of this chapter is to emphasize the importance of staying focused and maximizing your effort to get what you really want. The example set by Musashi in his training—before he reached his thirteenth birthday—is one of the most remarkable stories in the history of Japan's famed samurai class.

It is an example that should be emulated in today's world, but regrettably that is not the case, particularly in Japan. Young Japanese today are now poorly focused and desperately in need of a national identity. It is time we learned from Musashi and this book.

— *Michihiro Matsumoto*

In his *Book of Five Rings* Miyamoto Musashi makes two obvious points about goals: First, you must choose a goal before you can achieve it, and second, the more difficult and dangerous your goal is, the more effort you must put into achieving it.

Musashi's goal, which he established well before he reached his teens, was to become the best swordsman in his world. This would have been an ambitious goal at any time, but it was especially so in a world where swordsmanship was a matter of life and death for the class that ruled the country.

Musashi set out to be the best in a world that was already populated by many champion swordfighters who were obviously accomplished in the martial arts— demonstrated by the fact that they were still alive!

There are few, if any, goals in modern life that compare with the ones Musashi set for himself. But all achievement starts with goals, and Musashi emphasized that you should be ambitious in setting them. Ambitious goals will help you focus your energies, abilities, and actions to maximum effect.

CHAPTER TWO

Life-or-Death Discipline

The point of this chapter is innovation—a buzzword that venture capitalists love and an art that can mean the difference between success (life) and failure (death) in samurai terms. Google, You-tube, not to mention the Internet itself, did not come from big companies. They came from individuals who remained disciplined in their dedication to innovation; from individuals who did not have security blankets to catch them if they fell.

Musashi himself was obviously self-motivated to an incredibly degree, but an inquiring and innovative mind can be taught by example and by providing opportunities for the young to practice creativity—something now sorely lacking in the homes and schools around the world.

— *Michihiro Matsumoto*

Only incredible mental, physical, intellectual, and spiritual self-discipline can explain how Musashi was able to become the finest swordsman in the country while still in his teens. Although records of Musashi's childhood are scarce, it is obvious that he was strong-willed and extraordinarily self-disciplined from an early age.

In his *Book of Five Rings* Musashi wrote that he had no teacher, that he was entirely self-taught. His claim is creditable: If one of the proud master teachers in the institutionalized and ritualized training system of the samurai, which kept careful records, could have claimed him as a student, they surely would have.

It is obvious that by the time he was thirteen he was extremely accomplished, at least with a wooden staff, so much so that he had no qualms about challenging a seasoned warrior who had killed many men in one-on-one combat.

This is enough to make Musashi unique in the annals of the samurai, and rare in any setting. It suggests that, as he claims, his ambition formed very early and drove him to a level of self-discipline that seems incredible for a young boy on his own.

Perhaps the best way to illustrate the degree of self-discipline required would be to compare it with what young men and women training for the Olympics would go through if they tried to become champions without the support of coaches, national associations, or sponsors.

There is, of course, nothing new about the role of discipline in developing skills of any kind. But Musashi's accomplishments make it crystal clear that achieving incredible results requires incredible discipline—knowledge that can be applied in any endeavor.

CHAPTER THREE

Train to Win

The message here is Total Immersion. The percentage of young people who are motivated to the point that they totally immerse themselves in worthwhile pursuits is shockingly small. Far too many of them now spend nearly half of their waking hours propped up in front of the tube—something that their parents are responsible for.

And, yes, I still continue training in English—which is my sword, my weapon. I wake up every morning listening to English language Internet news. I call it my Total Immersion Method—my way of soaking myself in English everyday without going overseas. I don't believe in dumbing myself down by watching long hours of TV pap. Why? To win, I need ammunition—new words, new meanings, new uses!

— *Michihiro Matsumoto*

The fighting skills that Miyamoto Musashi and other samurai developed, like those of Olympic champions, did not come easily. Although Musashi claimed to have been self-trained, we can assume that he based his training on the models provided by the most accomplished samurai instructors of the day.

Their programs were based on a regime of training that began in early childhood; was engaged in for several hours a day, generally six days a week; and continued for many years.

The formal training began when boys reached the age of six or seven. Around the age of fifteen, at which time they became full-fledge warriors, one of the common rites of passage was beheading several men who were either condemned convicts or captured enemies— to get the "feel" of cutting off a head.

Once the samurai had mastered the different weapons in their arsenal, particularly the sword, their training was reduced to a few hours a day several times a week—and continued until they died or retired.

Even samurai who became full-time administrators continued to practice with the sword. Those of higher rank, including shoguns, retained masters to teach them and serve as sparring partners.

For *shugyosha* like Musashi, intense daily training continued throughout their active lives because their lives depended upon their skills. They did not train just to engage in tournaments for show. They trained to uphold their honor and reputations and to stay alive.

To succeed in today's world, you too must keep yourself in "fighting trim" through constant and continuing training. Like the samurai, you need both physical and psychological exercises to stay physically sharp and mentally alert. You also need to continue training in your "weapons"—the special skills and techniques required by your field of endeavor—to survive and prosper.

CHAPTER FOUR

Be Prepared

Musashi constantly harped on the eternal truth that being forewarned is being forearmed. Preparing yourself in advance for fighting or doing business is absolutely essential for success. I was once a TV Asahi anchorperson on a midnight program and before I took on the challenge I learned what it means to be a journalist—to be "combat ready" before going on each night. Before interviewing Larry King via satellite—someone I had never met—I read articles and books about him, and watched him in action on his own show.

To truly prepare in advance for a challenge requires both commitment and courage: the courage to undertake something new and the determination to see it through to the end. That was the way of the samurai, is a mindset that is rare in today's youth, and is a message made clear in this book.

— *Michihiro Matsumoto*

Musashi endlessly repeated that knowing yourself, knowing your weapons, knowing your surroundings and your enemy or competitor are all as important as your skill in fighting or in negotiating. He was a master at preparing for a battle beforehand because his goal was to never leave anything to chance.

He taught that the warrior with the prepared mind is favored, no matter what weapon is used. On a number of occasions he fought skilled swordsmen in death matches using just a piece of wood to demonstrate this principle. The fact that he was victorious against so many opponents says volumes about his preparation and points out the importance of being prepared.

Musashi prepared himself meticulously not only for situations that he expected, but also for unexpected turns of events, so that only his opponents would be surprised. It is easy to understand how important this is if, like Musashi, you risk your life with every fight. But it is just as important if you expect to be successful in any field that requires quick decisions and split-second actions.

The principle of advance preparation is obviously known to both business and military people in the West. But even though they know it is vital to their chances of success, it is clear that a significant percentage of them do not put it into practice.

It goes without saying that spending time meticulously preparing for meetings, competitions, or other important events will give you an invaluable advantage against less-prepared opponents. And the more prepared you are—for the unexpected as well as the expected—the more successful you will be.

CHAPTER FIVE

The Illusion of Form

Musashi did not believe in rigidly following *kamae* (kah-my)—the traditional stance at the beginning of a sword fight. He deliberately chose to think outside the box. The result was that in addition to fighting over sixty duels to the death before he was thirty, he participated in thousands of matches during his long life, never once losing. He taught that becoming fixed on a way or a style is the way to death—that fluidity is the way to life.

Absolute trust in *kamae* (always taking the same "ready" stance) can be fatal in a duel to the death or in business and diplomatic negotiations for that matter.

— *Michihiro Matsumoto*

In the introduction to his way of fighting, Musashi departs completely from the prevailing attitudes about the martial arts and the way they were practiced at that time. He dismisses the traditional attachment to form and styles, saying they are like concentrating on the blossoms of a fruit tree and ignoring the fruit. This would seem to substantiate his claim that, unlike other young male members of the warrior class, he had no teachers and followed no established style.

Musashi as much as accused many martial arts instructors of the day—particularly Buddhist priests who claimed that their way of fighting was given to them by the gods—of being frauds. He went on to say that the traditional martial arts forms that had been taught for centuries had become barriers that prevented martial artists from being able to see the realities of engaging another person in a swordfight, especially when it was a duel to the death.

Apparently because his way of looking at swordsmanship and his method of fighting were so unorthodox, he did not try to explain them until he was on his deathbed. His way of teaching was to demonstrate his method of fighting in training sessions and demonstrations, leaving it up to his opponents, students, and onlookers to learn from the experience and from viewing him in action.

There were many stories during his early life that he

himself was a fraud and that the victories he had won up to that time were flukes of one kind or another. On many occasions he was invited by fief lords and shogunate officials to engage them or one of their champions in demonstration bouts in the belief that he would be exposed as some kind of charlatan.

In over fifty years of dueling, fighting in wars, and demonstrating his techniques, beginning when he was only thirteen years old, Musashi never lost a single match. It is recorded that on one occasion the sword of an opponent cut a rent in the garment he was wearing—and that was the closest he ever got to suffering bodily harm.

The message that he taught over and over again, and in myriad ways, was that unfailing success in fighting and in any other endeavor is based on not being blinded by illusions—by grasping the essence of one's self, one's opponents or competitors, the task at hand, the circumstances of the physical location, and the surrounding environment. There is, of course, no better advice.

Despite his claim that he took nothing from the Buddhist scripts or any of the other teachings of the day, Musashi's outlook on life was pure Zen, which teaches how to recognize and deal with reality in a detached, objective way—minus the emotions that make life such a trial for so many people.

CHAPTER SIX

Absolute Integrity

What justice is to the Western world, *wa* (wah) or harmony is to Japanese society. Inazo Nitobe says in his great book *Bushido: The Soul of Japan*, that the foundation of the code of the samurai is justice. But the term justice is a word that hardly ever appears in a Japanese frame of reference, including moral standards. And no bilingual dictionaries that I know seem to do justice to it.

It takes a sharp sense and cultural awareness to get to the heart of the Japanese sense of morality. He refers it to as "Japanese etiquettes," enforced by law, by custom, and by the acute sense of shame the Japanese feel when they fail to live up to the embedded social standards—a sense of shame, instead of a sense of guilt.

It is the sharp eyes of others, rather than ambiguous conscience or justice, that make the Japanese behave. It is those prying eyes that keep the average Japanese (those who have not been de-Japanized by overseas experience) *Japanese* and abiding by the rules of Japanese etiquettes, which I refer as *wa* (harmony Japanese style), the anchor of our soul.

The unwritten and undefined *wa* remains the core or the magnetic center of the Japanese cultural ethos. The *wa* of Japan is the Japanese version of justice in disguise. As long as Japan has "it", even in reduced measure, the samurai spirit will survive.

— *Michihiro Matsumoto*

In his book *Bushido: The Soul of Japan*, Inazo Nitobe writes that the foundation of the code of samurai is justice—that nothing is more loathsome to a samurai than underhanded dealings and unjust behavior. He adds that the concept of justice is the power of deciding on a course of action in accordance with reason, without wavering, and in the words of a samurai, "to strike when it is right to strike and to die when it is right to die."

The level of integrity achieved in Japan during the reign of the samurai was unparalleled in history. The rules of the shogunate and the fief lords were clear and explicit. You followed the ethical standards that were the law of the land or you were punished, generally by a quick and often painful death.

Much of the morality that was prescribed during the samurai era regulated public behavior and was therefore visible for all to see. Morality was not based on religious precepts but on strict secular tenets designed to create a specific kind of harmony in Japanese society. This secular-based morality, now generally referred as "Japanese etiquette," was enforced by law, by custom, and by the acute sense of shame the Japanese felt when they failed to live up to these social standards.

By some measures, the traditional morality of the Japanese people has been significantly diluted since the introduction of democracy and individuality into the country after World War II. But by international standards, the Japanese as a whole are probably still the most moral people in the world.

How does such a strict standard of morality or integrity promote success? As in Musashi's time, adherence to moral and societal standards leaves no question as to the right way to act. With no ambiguity or uncertainty about behavior, competitors and combatants can focus on the task at hand. Along with other positive traits of the samurai character—discipline, honesty, loyalty, and perseverance—absolute integrity is critical to achieving success while upholding the standards of a moral society.

CHAPTER SEVEN

Train the Mind

The case for samurai-type education for the youth of the world is crystallized in this chapter—a system of physical and mental training that would instill discipline in the young people of today—the kind of discipline that resulted in the samurai committing suicide rather than being shamed.

Contemporary Japanese still carry a long sword for fighting and enforcing the law and a short sword for committing *hara-kiri* (hah-rah-kee-ree) or formal suicide—both in the form of apologies for "crimes" they may or may not have committed.

In certain circumstances the Japanese commit verbal *hara-kiri* to take responsibility for some misdeed, whether or not they were directly responsible. Among Japan's famous Yakuza gangsters cutting off a small finger was the traditional way of making a "very sincere" apology (to their bosses) for some infraction—a mild form of apology when compared to slicing open one's stomach.

Milder still is the Japanese custom of taking the blame for something by apologizing to the public. But in Japan's "shame culture" the shame of a public apology is very painful indeed, even though it may appear to Westerners to be a sham or token apology.

Until modern times, Japan's samurai did not hesitate to kill themselves at a moment's notice because they put honor above death. Unlike Japan's samurai of old, today's samurai businesspeople generally resort to committing professional suicide with an apology instead of the real thing with a sword.

— *Michihiro Matsumoto*

Musashi's main strength, as he said many times, was not in superior ability with weapons, but in using his mind to defeat his opponents. And it is obvious that at a very early age he trained his mind as vigorously as he did his body.

Except for the automatic functions of the body, the mind is the "software" that directs physical actions. Something causes the mind to "push a key" and the body reacts in a certain way. But this software is not built into the higher, civilized levels of the brain. It has to be "uploaded" through mental and physical training, preferably from early childhood.

Once this software has been "wired" into the brain it is not easy to change or erase, but it can be altered by additional, ongoing training. In other words, training the body can change the software that runs the brain, altering the way we think and act.

Early in their history the Japanese recognized and understood these fundamental principles of psychology and physiology, and they created a system of customs and rituals that were specifically designed to train both the mind and the body. In some of these practices, including the skills developed by the samurai, the physical training generally started before the individual was mature enough—intellectually, emotionally, and spiritually—to make a commitment to such an intensive program.

That is where the system of masters, mentors, and teachers—or in Musashi's case, extreme self-discipline —came in.

Both the physical and mental training of samurai youth began around the age of six or seven. The art of the sword and other weapons was studied and practiced daily for several hours.

By the time samurai youth were seven or eight years old it was as important to program their minds as it was to temper their bodies, if not more so. Their mental "software" had to be changed to provide the discipline necessary to achieve the goals of the training.

Young samurai boys were psychologically and philosophically programmed to be diligent, responsible, and fearless, and to look upon death as no more than a transition to another level of existence. They were trained to believe that death was preferable to failure and shame. Part of their training was to go to the execution grounds and practice cutting the heads and limbs off of criminals who had just been executed. More dedicated fathers and trainers provided the trainees with live criminals to behead.

At the age of fifteen they became full-fledged warriors and were required by the code of the samurai to wear two swords at all times when they were in public—a long sword, for fighting and enforcing the law, and a short sword to be used to commit *harakiri* (hah-rah-kee-ree)—that is, to kill themselves by slicing their stomach open—a custom that was so common that finally in the early 1600s the Tokugawa Shogunate issued an edict prohibiting the practice.

This mental training gave the samurai the edge—and the certainty—they needed to act effectively and decisively in difficult situations. It proved to be an invaluable aid not just in combat, but in their roles as leaders and rulers as well.

Musashi clearly responded to this psychological training with exceptional diligence and made use of it in all of his endeavors. His success offers invaluable direction for succeeding at today's challenges.

If you are an athlete, don't neglect to train your mind as well as your body. Make sure your training includes developing the mental discipline necessary

CHAPTER EIGHT

Clear the Mind

In this chapter it is made obvious that Musashi apparently had no ego at all—a factor that played an extraordinary role in his incredible drive to continue studying and practicing swordsmanship all his life and to regard every opponent, no matter how inept, as someone he could learn from.

Zen, the philosophy Musashi followed, teaches one that the primary obstacle to enlightenment and wisdom is ego—the selfish and glorified sense of self most people have. Musashi was so ego-less that it drove some of his friends and most of his enemies to distraction—giving him a great advantage over his enemies.

This is a lesson that should be demonstrated by adults and taught to children from a very young age.

— Michihiro Matsumoto

One feature of the samurai's psychological training that Musashi emphasized was developing the Zen-based capability for "clearing the mind"—that is, eliminating the chorus of thoughts and images that constantly swirl in the brain and interfere with the coherent and efficient function of both the brain and the body.

The most common Zen way of clearing the mind is *zazen* (zah-zen), or "seated meditation." There is indisputable evidence, in both practical applications and clinical research, that meditation or "clearing the mind" improves your ability to think more clearly and function more effectively.

However, getting control of the mind is far more difficult to do than you might imagine. One Japanese master, after a lifetime of training in meditation, said that during his entire life he had succeeded in having complete control of his mind for only three seconds.

From the fourteenth century on, all samurai were taught to meditate regularly as a way of strengthening control over their minds and enhancing their sensory perceptions. Musashi obviously mastered the Zen way of meditating, and attributed much of his success in battle and in the arts to this simple practice.

There are many occasions when turning the mind off is the best thing to do. If your body has been sufficiently trained, it can then do what it is supposed to do. In Japanese, this state is known as *mushin* (muu-sheen), or "no mind," as well as *muga* (muu-gah), meaning "no ego." According to Zen Buddhism, once a person is in a state of *mushin/muga*, accomplishing a task is as easy as thinking it.

Musashi tried to totally empty his mind of all distractions—even the various forms and techniques of fighting that he had mastered! He wanted to be absolutely free to use whatever approach, tactic, or technique that came naturally to the situation at hand. His philosophy was that every movement should be absolutely natural to the mind and body so that it can be accomplished without having to plan or think about it. This is, of course, the mark of a champion athlete or a master of any art, including painting, juggling, or using a bow and arrow.

Meditation has long been a cultural custom in Japan, practiced by most people at some time or another, and regularly by priests, tea masters, artists, landscape gardeners, potters, warriors, and businesspeople. Some of modern-day Japan's most successful businessmen meditate to enhance their decision-making and management skills. A few Japanese corporations even require all of their managers to spend time in temples meditating under the strict supervision of Buddhist priests.

A Japanese Olympic diving champion who had been performing under par during the early qualifying performances turned everything around on her last two attempts and came through like the champion she was. When asked how she had done it, she replied: "I turned my mind off and just did what came natural [to my body]."

Most people today are so caught up in the chaos and cacophony of modern life and work that they are unable to use even the smallest percentage of the power of their own minds.

It therefore goes without saying that people would benefit from meditating. But it should especially be a part of the training and the regular routine of all people in leadership or management positions—in business, in politics, and in the military.

This is another area in which a very small change in lifestyle—fifteen to twenty minutes a day of meditating—could have far-reaching effects. If nothing else, it would improve your mental and physical health and contribute to a longer and more tranquil life. If meditation doesn't work for you, develop your own means of "clearing" your mind so that you can focus more lucidly and act more effectively.

CHAPTER NINE

The Power of Emptiness

The lesson in this chapter is the power of selflessness and an uncluttered mind. Takamori Saigo, who has been described as Japan's equivalent of Abraham Lincoln, was a passionate man of no personal ambition. He was an amazing magnet, attracting over 30,000 young men who were willing to die with him for his cause.

Where did his power come from? It came from the power, the charisma, of emptiness—from the fact that he had absolutely no illusions about his importance and no ambitions for himself...only for the well-being of Japan. As we say, he was a man with a big *hara* (a man whose mind was empty of personal desires and illusions).
                                    — *Michihiro Matsumoto*

Musashi's mental training went beyond clearing the mind of extraneous thoughts and preconceived notions. His point was that a completely empty mind made it possible for one to respond spontaneously to the circumstances at hand, and gave him a special power over his opponents. In fact, his fighting style was based as much on what he called "the power of emptiness" as on his skill with weapons. A point that he made over and over was the importance of not letting the mind interfere with one's actions—a weakness that most of us are familiar with.

He said this factor was especially important when fighting more than one person at the same time. It was especially vital when facing a large group of fighters who have attacked you and are determined to cut you down. His secret was to completely empty his mind of any second thoughts, any fear, or anything else, and let his body do what he had trained it to do.

Musashi gave *more* credit to the power of emptiness than he did to his ability with the sword—which, as he noted, was something any other well-trained warrior could match. His point was that to do something perfectly, whether in fighting or in painting or any other art, it was necessary to let your well-trained body and your subconscious direct your actions. This Zen Buddhist concept was at the heart of the extraordinary skill of many of Japan's master artists and craftsmen—from painters to garden designers.

Again, this is something that great competitors know instinctively and practice unconsciously. Where business and other affairs are concerned, the point is to know your subject absolutely, practice its execution until it is automatic, and then proceed without any doubts or mental reservations.

CHAPTER TEN

Learn from Your Opponents

There is no evidence that Musashi based any of his fighting techniques on the way a praying mantis stalks and attacks its victims, but in this chapter Boyé attributes to Musashi all of the techniques and skills used by this extraordinary insect—acute observation, quick adaptation, camouflage, and then an attack that is so swift it is virtually invisible to the intended victim. Both Musashi and preying mantids (pun intended) learned from their opponents. The message in this chapter is that achieving something great, such as surviving a death duel, you must be willing to risk all.

— *Michihiro Matsumoto*

Musashi developed an incredible ability to really perceive the things he looked at—not just physical objects, but movements and patterns, like those of the sun, animals, birds, water, and people. He studied these until their essence—including how they manifested themselves—became clear to him. He then incorporated what he had learned into his approach to fighting.

In Musashi's descriptions of his encounters, he explains in detail the weaknesses of his opponents and what he learned from them. His remarkable powers of observation made it possible for him to detect the fighting style of his opponents in a matter of seconds and absorb anything from their style that he considered worthwhile. He could then adjust his own style to overwhelm them, usually in a matter of seconds.

It was apparently this ability to observe, learn, and adapt nearly instantly that made it possible for Musashi to become an unbeatable swordsman without having a tutor.

The obvious lesson here: Study your opponents and competitors carefully. Know their strengths and their weaknesses precisely. Learn from them, adapt your approach to take advantage of their weaknesses, and then defeat them before they realize that you have changed your tactics.

CHAPTER ELEVEN

Pay Attention to Details

In this chapter Boyé focuses on the role that details played in Musashi's incredible success as a duelist. It is often said that the devil is in the details, but it is common for people to gloss over the smaller details, especially when big projects or major programs are concerned.

Musashi developed a kind of 4-dimensional skill in evaluating an opponent, the lay of the land, the weather, the time of day and more, in his fights to the death. As he noted numerous times big things will naturally be taken care of...it is almost always the small things that trip people up and bring on failure. In his case, failure to take details into account could have meant immediate death.

Agreeing to agree on principles first and then discuss the details later is often a recipe for failure, especially in Japan...and this is something that Westerners should be aware of and take seriously.

— *Michihiro Matsumoto*

Among the training precepts recorded by the samurai-scholars of the fifteenth and sixteenth centuries, the importance of paying special attention to small details was high on the list. One of the more popular axioms of the samurai reminded them to treat great things casually and small things seriously—as if their life depended on these details, as it often did. In his treatise on his way of fighting, Musashi emphasized that paying attention to small details was one of the most critical aspects of winning any battle, or succeeding in any enterprise.

Musashi made the point that people who fail in large enterprises often do so because they ignore the little things, or leave them to people who are not absolutely dependable. He pointed out that in battles to the death, warriors who did not personally maintain their weapons, who had not studied their own strengths and weaknesses and developed plans to either use them or compensate for them, or who failed to study their opponents carefully were not likely to live long.

Throughout his lifetime, Musashi practiced his philosophy through constant study and training, never assuming that he had learned everything he needed to know, or that the little details would take care of themselves.

Present-day businesspeople who fail may not be in danger of losing their lives, but if they do not under-

CHAPTER TWELVE

The Power of Silence

Once again, Boyé's focus here is on the similarity between Musashi's way of victory over his opponents and the way praying mantids stalk and attack their victims. Unlike other insects they make no noise at all and are virtually invisible until they spring their attack.

Musashi's use of the power of silence is still characteristic of Japanese businesspeople in negotiating situations. Their prolonged silences often drive foreigners (especially Americans) up the wall because they cannot figure what is going on, and typically end up losing their perspective and weakening their position.

Many of Musashi's opponents were so upset by his nonchalance and apparent disinterest in them and in the situation at hand that they lost their cool, and their lives.

The point is, silence is often far more powerful than words, and learning how to use it is a valuable asset.

— *Michihiro Matsumoto*

To the average Westerner, silence is the absence of sound, has no form or essence, and performs no function of its own. In the traditional Japanese mind-set, however, silence has both form and an essence, and it plays a vital role in achieving control of the mind, in the creative process and in communicating with nature and with people.

Musashi was a master at using silence as one of his most powerful weapons. He was silent most of his life, in part, perhaps, because he spent so much of his life alone. Not only did he not boast about his accomplishments, when he did talk or write, he played them down and spoke only in the humblest of terms. His thoughts therefore remained unknown to most of the people he met in his lifetime.

This had both positive and negative effects. On the one hand, his silence created an aura of mystery about him that was often an asset. It made some people curious to meet him or afraid to challenge him, which he often used to his advantage. On the other hand, it made many people think he was not altogether right in the head. They would speak disparagingly of him— saying that since he spent so much time traveling, without so much as a change of clothing, he was not fit to be welcomed into any home.

Whatever the case, his manner resulted in people viewing him with strong emotions. Some regarded him as a fool. Others regarded him as someone who did not behave properly and was therefore neither a worthy opponent nor an acceptable guest.

During many of his encounters with men determined to kill him Musashi never spoke, and he often behaved as if they were not there. This lack of any sign of emotion or interest unnerved or puzzled his opponents, giving him an advantage before the first move. He either cut them down before they got their wits together, or he killed them when they forgot to be cautious and rushed in to strike him.

The lesson for businesspeople is clear: While there can be great advantages to sharing information with your business partners, it can also be extremely important not to reveal too much about your assets, your plans, or your intentions in advance—something that present-day Japanese businessmen do automatically.

CHAPTER THIRTEEN

Change the Rules of Engagement

The lesson in this chapter is the role that psychology plays in human relations, particularly in business negotiations and in war. Musashi has been accused by some of playing dirty in the most famous duel he ever fought, but his fights were not sport—they were fights to the death.

Musashi did not fight dirty. He ignored the conventional protocol rules that had become embedded in the samurai code—being on time for a duel, announcing your name and so on—but he knew you did not stay alive by treating an adversary like a guest in your home or office.

On the other hand, debating is a game played by rules, and there are rules of engagement in business, but if you do not know the rules that the other side is playing by you had better be a fast learner—or very lucky.

Negotiating is an art that differs in different cultures. It is not a science. The art in a confrontational context involves style, class, character and panache, and all that stuff. Musashi simply cut through all of that to the core of the goal—kill his adversary as quickly and as cleanly as possible.

In the case of this famous fight, Musashi stacked the cards in his favor with a simple psychological ploy that might be thought of as less than genteel, and maybe even rude, but it was not dirty.

Such ploys would not be appropriate for business or diplomatic purposes, but in war, especially wars of terrorism, they have their place.

— *Michihiro Matsumoto*

Adhering precisely to a highly stylized and formal etiquette was (and is) the basis for Japanese morality. During the long reign of the samurai class (1192–1868) failure to conform to the prescribed etiquette was, in effect, a moral and a secular sin that often was punishable by death. There was a precise way of doing everything, from the most mundane actions to the most exalted ceremonies and rituals—including *harakiri* and engaging in duels.

Adherence to a strict, formal etiquette is still the standard of behavior among virtually all adults in Japan, and it continues to distinguish the Japanese from other people. Young Japanese, influenced by the Western concepts of individuality and independence, typically ignore the traditional etiquette when interacting among themselves in personal situations, but in order to be accepted into the adult world, they must conform to the traditional etiquette in speech as well as in their physical behavior. Japan's traditional culture remains so strong in the adult world that it is not likely to disappear any time soon.

One of Musashi's favorite and most effective weapons was the power of unexpected behavior. This was an especially powerful weapon because Japanese standards of behavior were precisely prescribed forms that had been programmed into his opponents from infancy. His adversaries were often so shocked by his unconventional and "non-conforming" behavior that they lost their presence of mind, and their lives.

Musashi was described as a wayward youth who often misbehaved, so he obviously grew up being a maverick as far as the detailed choreography of Japanese etiquette was concerned. He also obviously observed how unexpected (un-Japanese) behavior upset everyone, and he made this knowledge part of his arsenal of tactics in fighting.

For example, Musashi carried and used two swords—a long one and a short one, and called his way of fighting *Niten* (nee-tane), "Two Heavens," or "Two Swords Style." His skill was such, however, that in most of his later fights to the death he used wooden rather than steel swords—something that infuriated his opponents because they regarded such behavior as treating them and the exalted code of the samurai with contempt.

The power of the unexpected was dramatically demonstrated by two of Musashi's most famous duels—

one in Kyoto when he was twenty-one, where he killed several well-known warriors over a three-day period, and the another when he met an opponent, by pre-arrangement, on a beach on a secluded island (known as "Boat Island" because of its silhouette).

On the first day of the Kyoto affair, Musashi showed up late for an appointed duel with the head of a group of some one hundred warriors of a leading clan. His meticulously mannered opponent became furious, losing his cool and then his life. Musashi then arranged to fight the leader's brother, who was second in command of the group, on the following day. He showed up late again, with the same result—he killed the infuriated and overwrought warrior immediately.

On the third day, Musashi was supposed to fight the son of the man he killed the first day. This time he arrived early, taking the over one hundred clan members who had gathered to take revenge by surprise. Jumping out of the early morning mist into the crowd of warriors before they got their wits about them, Musashi instantly cut down his designated opponent and then began herding the group of warriors before him as if they were sheep, killing one after the other until the remainder of the group turned and fled.

In the "Boat Island" duel, which occurred when he was twenty-nine (in 1612), Musashi arrived at the island some two hours late. He had deliberately slept late, eaten a leisurely breakfast, and then carved a wooden sword out of an oar before being rowed out to the island.

His opponent, Kojiro Sasaki, a huge warrior much feared for his prowess with a sword and his reputation for having killed many men in duels, was so furious at Musashi for "breaking the rules" that he rushed toward him, throwing away his scabbard at the same time.

Musashi yelled out, "You have already lost!" He evaded the enraged warrior's slashing sword and struck him on the head with a blow that knocked him to the ground. Sasaki was unconscious but still alive. Musashi struck him a second time, this time on the chest, killing him.

This lesson applies to competition of all kinds—unexpected behavior can disrupt your opponents' most carefully developed plans and give you the opening you need to press your advantage.

CHAPTER FOURTEEN

The Power of Fear

Musashi's technique of doing something suddenly that shocked an adversary and filled him with fear is not something I recommend for business situations but in war, making your opponents fearful of you is a well-known stratagem.

China's famed military expert Sun Tzu made a special point of the use of fear in his famous book *The Art of War*, written in the 6th century B.C. Ancient Greek and Roman military strategists used the art of confusing and frightening their enemies by making themselves appear far larger and more formidable than in reality, the way various animals and birds do by rearing up on their hind legs or spreading their wings. The Greeks, Romans, and most other military forces were also experts at creating shocking sounds or spectacles that rattled their enemies and made them more vulnerable.

The lesson in this insightful chapter is more for the warrior than the businessperson, but it also works in many sports and can be a useful tool in personal encounters with others.

— *Michihiro Matsumoto*

It goes without saying that fear can be upsetting and debilitating, and can be used to make powerful opponents more vulnerable to attack. Musashi was a master at using fear to weaken his opponents. Sometimes he would remain silent and unmoving, making his opponents anxious about him and his fighting style. Then he would crush them with such speed and violence that he seemed to be possessed by some demon. On other occasions he would suddenly lunge at an opponent and let out a shriek to startle them, making it possible for him to cut them down before they had time to react.

Musashi was so accomplished that, according to eyewitness accounts, he sometimes caught the sword of an opponent between the palms of his bare hands as it descended toward his head—an incredible feat that was one of the reasons why he became so feared, respected, and praised during his lifetime. This tactic of catching an opponent's sword as it descends is a mainstay of some of the heroes of Japan's famous samurai movies, commonly referred to as *chambara* (chahm-bah-rah)—a word that refers to the noise made by clashing swords. The chambara films are the Japanese equivalent of American Westerns, with their gunslinger heroes.

Musashi always had an additional edge—his opponents did not know what fighting style he was going to use and therefore had to fear attacks that would leave them defenseless. Moreover, the fact that he had killed a number of famous warriors before he was out of his teens surely added some measure of fear in all of his subsequent opponents. Using fear as a tactic was certainly not something that Musashi originated, but few have used it with more skill and success, especially in one-on-one encounters where one of the combatants was going to die.

Frightening your opponents might not be appropriate for a businessperson—it might even be a great way to lose business—but a certain level of intimidation can be invaluable in negotiations or competition. The lesson here is to take advantage of any reasonable leverage you can bring to a contest. As is well known to many athletes, anything you can do to rattle your opponent gives you the upper hand.

CHAPTER FIFTEEN

Confuse Your Opponent

Many of the techniques Musashi used to kill his adversaries were just plain common sense—something that he often raised to the level of rare wisdom. He knew intuitively that people are more vulnerable when they are confused, and he used this stratagem in many different ways. He often said that it was far better to defeat an opponent with your mind than with a sword—a lesson that can be applied to business, sports, and war.

— *Michihiro Matsumoto*

Musashi used the power of confusion with deadly efficiency during many of his duels to the death and with the hundreds of men he later fought without intending to kill them. It is obvious that individuals who are suddenly confused or thrown off guard are not in full command of their faculties and can make mistakes that they wouldn't ordinarily make. All Musashi had to do was get an opponent to hesitate for one or two seconds. That was all the time he needed to strike a fatal blow.

One of his fighting tactics was what he called "the rhythm of striking an opponent in one count." This was assuming a pose with his sword that made it appear that he was vulnerable to attack, resulting in the opponent concentrating on the opening. Musashi then cut the opponent down in one quick movement before he had time to draw his sword back.

On other occasions, he lowered his sword as if he had forgotten where he was. Again, his surprised opponent, seeing what he thought was an opening, would spring forward recklessly, only to be met by a move so fast he was unable to dodge or block it.

Of course, confusing and misleading opponents is a classic tactic in virtually any kind of engagement. The less time they have to prepare themselves, the more likely you are to succeed. In military conflicts especially, using false starts, apparent inaction, or dramatic

CHAPTER SIXTEEN

The Mind as a Weapon

Another thing that should be mentioned in this chapter is the role that Zen meditation played in the training and lives of the samurai. The most crucial thing in whether or not a samurai survived a one-on-one duel or a gang fight was his ability to avoid being distracted or becoming flustered in any way.

The samurai practiced Zen meditation as a key means of developing an extraordinary ability to focus on a single point as well as on a variety of things at the same time, depending on the circumstances at hand.

No matter what approach Musashi took in his hundreds of bouts, he never lost control of his mind. He remained focused like a laser—a skill achieved by engaging in meditation for lengthy periods of time throughout his life.

This is the kind of concentration that is characteristic of people who are extraordinarily successful in business and other pursuits.

— *Michihiro Matsumoto*

In his treatise on fighting, Musashi repeatedly said that it was far better to defeat your opponent with your mind than with a weapon—meaning that it was better to first "strike" with the mind to weaken or virtually disarm an opponent and then, if necessary, use your sword to finish the job.

He used a variety of ruses that gave him a major psychological advantage in his fights. These included arriving late for a fight, arriving early for a fight, not using the expected sword, saying nothing at all or saying something that would rattle his opponents, and so on. These were all simple things that he knew would upset his opponents and distract them from the battle at hand.

On one famous occasion, Musashi approached a skilled swordsman with a stick of firewood instead of a sword and killed him with a single blow to the head. It is hard to say, from this distance, exactly why Musashi was able to kill the warrior in a split second with a piece of wood. It may have been because he was so fast and so deadly that his opponent didn't have time to defend himself, or he may have been so rattled by Musashi's unorthodox weapon that he was unable to function.

Musashi obviously understood at a very young age that breaking your opponents' mental concentration was one of the best ways to weaken them. Again, behaving in such a way that his opponents could not anticipate what he was going to do was one of his most successful tactics.

Of course, this kind of psychological warfare has always been a part of war—from shouting and beating on drums to broadcasting loud music and propaganda to dropping leaflets from the air. Modern-day warriors who resort to the force of arms in actual fighting or confrontations may be taking on their opponents the hard way. They should not hesitate to improvise and do the unexpected. They might find that the edge they gain actually reduces the chances of a deadly, destructive conflict.

CHAPTER SEVENTEEN

See What Cannot Be Seen

In this chapter Boyé describes Musashi's use of his "all-seeing eyes" to give him an advantage over his adversaries.

The lesson to both business managers and government leaders is clear—if they do not see clearly all of the elements that make up a threat or scenario they are likely to miss something that is vitally important and fail in their efforts. Throughout history there has been a long list of both companies and countries that have failed to learn this lesson, and have suffered the consequences.

Today the greatest failing of businesspeople, politicians, and diplomats is that their narrow view of others cannot discern the cultural differences of people. They see the world in only one or two dimensions.

— *Michihiro Matsumoto*

Japanese movies about the feats of samurai often portray the hero "seeing" things that the average person cannot see, and somehow "knowing" the exact location of an object or enemy that is hidden behind walls or other obstacles. Some of these portrayals are obviously exaggerated, but it is a matter of record that many Zen priests and samurai warriors honed their senses to the point that they could, in fact, see and hear things that were invisible and inaudible to others.

The founder of Zen, the Indian priest Bodhidharma, is said to have reached the point that he could hear the conversations of ants. (He sat before a wall—meditating—for nine years!) It is also said that some warriors could hear the difference between the rustle of silk garments in a distant hallway and fluttering leaves outside a house.

Musashi practiced meditating regularly and made much of being able "to see what cannot be seen" in his instructions to his disciples, so we can assume that he himself had developed his "extrasensory perception" to a high level. Musashi used a Zen Buddhist term meaning "to look through" in his treatise. The term he used also means to understand the essence of what is being looked at. With this understanding, one can react correctly to things or events both near and far.

The point here is not to spend years meditating in order to have superman eyes and ears, but to reach the

CHAPTER EIGHTEEN

Don't Get Stuck on One Style

As Musashi noted, letting go of a form or style, once you have acquired it, is easier said than done. Doing what comes naturally as circumstances dictate is even harder. Musashi apparently never got hung up on form in the first place and it was this rare insight that helped make him such a formidable opponent.

The Japanese military failed to understand and follow this principle in the Pacific War. They got stuck on "form" and lost the war.

I for one followed the advice of Musashi, my mentor, and refuse to abide by any customary form to study English, not relying on textbooks or going overseas to immerse myself in English environments.

What did I do then? I listened to Master Musashi and did the unorthodox, by losing myself in the English language sword and using it entirely in Japan. My technique was to use logical English as my weapon in a debate format...debating with all of the will and ferocity of a samurai engaged in a battle to the death.

I became Musashi with a two-way language sword, a gunslinger who shoots words instead of bullets. Boyé has described me as the most dangerous man in Japan because I ask "why"? a taboo question in Japan because "why" is a straight shot.

So how do I survive? The secret is *haragei*—built-in circular logic. *Haragei* takes a circular path like a boomerang. It takes *haragei* logic, or prelogic, to heal a person's ego injured by the whys and the becauses in life.

— *Michihiro Matsumoto*

One of Musashi's primary goals in traveling about the country and meeting other samurai in duels and in demonstration bouts (called "comparisons of technique") was to observe and learn their different styles of fighting. The more familiar he became with the variety of fighting tactics, the less likely he was to see a style he hadn't seen before or didn't know how to defeat.

In his years of observing the behavior of other samurai in training and in his encounters with dozens of them in duels, Musashi discovered that virtually all of them followed a precise form in their combat—from the way they placed and moved their feet to how they held and used their swords. These men, obviously, were conditioned mentally and physically to precisely follow the fighting styles they had been taught. Musashi realized that this was a major weakness that left the warriors vulnerable to opponents who understood their style of fighting and could respond with tactics designed to counter them.

Musashi made it his practice to never depend on any particular form, even those that he had perfected. His approach was to change to any style that would give him an advantage over his opponent.

Whether in battle, business, or sports, people tend to go with what they have been taught and what has worked for them in the past—even if it is not working in the present. The moral, of course, is don't get stuck on any one way of doing things. You are more likely to succeed if you change your tactics the moment it becomes obvious that the old ways are not working.

Musashi's message is simple: Once you have mastered your weapons and tactics, forget about form and do what comes naturally in response to the circumstances at hand.

CHAPTER NINETEEN

The Importance of Flexibility

In his book *Lateral Think* author Edward de Bono compared the "water logic" of the Japanese with the "rock logic" of Westerners—a legacy of Socrates. His theory opened my eyes to alternative logics, namely those of wind and fire.

In debate, a rock battle, is fire, *haragei*, the most non-confrontational form of interaction, is water. It does not follow man-made rules; it follows the water's nature logic. Yes means no and no means yes. Letting things flow like water provides you with infinite flexibility, giving *haragei* extraordinary power.

Musashi says become your enemy...and perhaps that is the best way to combat the fear of your enemy. Instead of putting your feet in the shoes of your enemies, put yourself in their *hara*—their stomachs...the better to communicate with them across cultural and racial lines.

In modern-day parlance "water logic" might be equated with fuzzy thinking…which is another way of saying holistic thinking, because it takes into account many things, including things that cannot be seen.

In the short term those who use the one-dimensional linear thinking that is characteristic of the Western world may win out, but in the long term the final winners will be the holistic thinkers.

— *Michihiro Matsumoto*

"Water" was one of the "five rings" making up the foundation of Musashi's fighting strategy and tactics. He chose water because it is one of the most flexible of all things in nature, conforming itself instantly and without effort to whatever shape it encounters. Moreover, water moves in the direction of least resistance without any effort whatsoever, and it eventually overcomes even the most powerful barrier. Musashi also made a special point of observing that when one's efforts are blocked and progress cannot be made against an opponent, one should imitate water that has been constrained behind a dam that suddenly collapses and rushes forward with incredible speed and power.

He taught that the mind of the samurai should be "like water"—the epitome of flexibility, able to change instantly to conform to and take advantage of any circumstance. Flexibility was, in fact, at the core of virtually everything that Musashi taught. He went further than advising his disciples to "be" flexible in fighting; he said that they should "absorb" flexibility into their minds as well as their bodies so that it came naturally to them without them having to think about it. Only this way, Musashi continued, can one avoid being surprised or caught off guard by anyone or anything.

He added that the frame of mind for one who has mastered flexibility is serenity or tranquility and that one of the key assets of the master swordsman is a tranquil mind. The lessons for people in the modern world are obvious.

CHAPTER TWENTY

Make Sure You See the Big Picture

Most of us tend to look at a picture, rather than *the whole* picture. Musashi taught that it was imperative that you see *the whole* picture before making any decision. No wonder he never lost a single match in his life and became known as the invisible sword master. His words of wisdom continue to echo across time and cultural lines.

A one-dimensional picture may give you the tactics you need for your immediate needs, whereas *the whole* picture gives you the distant view critical for creating and following a long-term strategy.

Seasoned observers first look at the total picture before writing a piece, and then they look at other pictures to flesh out their views. The lesson in this chapter is to make sure you view things with wide-angle eyes.

— *Michihiro Matsumoto*

Musashi realized that everything in nature, including the affairs of men, is in a constant state of flux—that nothing remains the same from one instant to the next. He sometimes compared the human mind with the water in a stream: It looks the same but it is always moving. (As we've seen, Water was one of the five symbols he used in his *Book of Five Rings*.)

In Musashi's philosophy, one was to keep an "open mind." He meant this not just in the general sense of being open to new ideas but in the specific moment-to-moment sense of not letting your mind focus on any one idea, feeling, object, or situation to the point where it distracts you from the events right in front of you.

One of Musashi's most effective tactics was to avoid focusing solely on an opponent's face, body, or weapon, because this prevented him from seeing the whole scene. His goal was to use his eyes like a wide-angle camera lens, allowing him to see everything in the immediate area. He was able to "see" himself, his opponent, and their surroundings as if he were viewing them from outside his own body, from an angle that allowed him to see the whole scene.

Musashi thus became as much a spectator as a participant in his battles. It is well known that spectators can see the weaknesses and mistakes made by fighters (and others) and recognize opportunities far more clearly than the participants themselves.

Another of his tactics was to never "stop the mind" —that is, to never focus on one thing long enough to prevent him from seeing everything else that was going on at the same time. He said that focusing the mind (his actual words were "putting the mind in one place") raised the risk of "falling into one-sidedness."

He maintained that your mind and your vision should be perfectly free to flow as water does, expanding and contracting to meet the circumstances of the moment. This understanding was crucial to Musashi's success as a warrior and his survival into old age.

In today's world, this means not focusing too much on the task at hand. This may sound paradoxical, given Musashi's instructions to pay careful attention to the details, but in fact these are just different ways of making the same point.

Musashi's commonsense suggestion was that we must also pay careful attention to events or situations seemingly in the background or on the periphery if we want to completely understand what is happening around us. Without this attention to the "edges" of situations, we are at risk of being blind-sided by threats or events we do not see coming.

CHAPTER TWENTY-ONE

Use Time as a Weapon

This chapter contains one of the most important lessons that Boyé has gleaned from Musashi, as it deals with the most quintessential part of Japanese concept of *ma* (mah), which may be translated as "a pregnant pause."

In its full Japanese context *ma* is not just a distance between objects or the interval of time between events. It is alive. It "breathes" shallow and deep, depending on the persons or parties involved. *Ma* is never empty. It is full of emotional content.

Make the animate *ma* "cry," and you'll be regarded as an inanimate human in Japan. You no longer fit in the *ma*-filled society of Japan. If you cannot feel the *ma* in Japanese society you cannot succeed in any relationship, business or social.

Those who are really serious about communicating clearly and fully in their dealings with the Japanese must learn how to use *ma*.

— *Michihiro Matsumoto*

The idea that "time is money" developed in Europe following the Industrial Revolution, when financiers began to establish businesses to make a profit and people began to work for wages. But long before that era, linear-thinking Westerners looked at time as something that stretched out before them in more or less a straight line, as something that could be measured in seconds, minutes, hours, days, and that if not used, it was wasted.

The traditional Japanese, by comparison, thought of time as a circle. All things came and went and were not measured by a clock ticking off seconds, minutes, and hours but by the seasons and other natural cycles. Instead of trying to do more things faster, the Japanese were more inclined to slow things down and do them better.

As a result, the Japanese build "space" or "time gaps" into whatever project they are engaged in, especially in business and political negotiations. This allows time for the two sides to rest, to clarify, strengthen, or reaffirm their positions. These time gaps are generally not planned or even acknowledged. They are taken for granted because they are built into the culture.

Since the Japanese see time differently from Westerners, they do not see these time gaps, called *ma* (mah) in Japanese, as "empty." They see them as part of the process of communicating, negotiating, and reaching consensus. Or they may be used as a tactic to table or block a proposal or project.

Musashi also used time as a weapon, but his approach was exactly the opposite of the traditional Japanese way. Instead of slowing things down, as others expected him to, he sped them up. He acted with such speed that he became almost invisible to his opponents, gaining an incomparable advantage.

He was able to capitalize on his opponents' assumptions or expectations about time to catch them off guard. In today's world, such cultural "assumptions" are often very subtle and may be difficult to detect, much less take advantage of. But a thorough knowledge of your opponent's cultural background and expectations can be invaluable in any kind of competition—and especially so in war.

CHAPTER TWENTY-TWO

Never Stop Learning

One of the primary strengths of Japan is its "shame culture." Unlike Americans and their guilt culture—which is easily concealed—the Japanese fear public shame more than anything else.

The Japanese are constantly resorting to *hansei-kai* (hahn-say-kie), or "soul-search sessions to learn from mistakes," in order to avoid being shamed—and this is at the heart of the Japanese obsession with *kaizen* (kie-zen) or "continuous improvement" in all things.

Boyé rightly uses the words "continuous learning" to hammer home the point that in Japan continuous learning and improvement is a life-long *michi* (me-chee), path or way. Japan's present-day samurai businessmen strive not just for perfection, they strive for continuous perfection, which is altogether different.

Speaking for myself, being a believer like Musashi in
continuous learning, I have never given up my life-long
pursuit of achieving "perfect English." Some people laugh
at me and say I am chasing rainbows. But I don't care and
I don't quit!

As founder of a school of philosophy based on
Musashi's concept of continuous learning, I argue that it
takes Zen and Bushido (The Way of the Warrior) to see
both English learning and swordplay as one and the
same. Both call for undivided attention and continuity.

— *Michihiro Matsumoto*

The concept of continuous learning throughout one's
lifetime has gained considerable cachet in the United
States and elsewhere in recent times. But we are still far
behind the Japanese, and it often shows.

The concept of continuous learning came to Japan
along with a wide range of arts and crafts that were
imported from China and Korea between 400 and 700
ad. These imports were accompanied by the master-
apprentice approach to teaching and training. Training
in all skills was manual, intellectual, philosophical,
and spiritual, and it continued for up to thirty years or
more in some of the more demanding arts and crafts.
For the Japanese, the practice of learning over a long
period of time became an integral part of their lifestyle
and a measure of their cultural expectations.

The advent of the samurai period in 1192 gave new

impetus to the concept of continuous learning. The samurai had to continue honing their physical and mental combat skills throughout their active years as warriors because their lives depended on it.

By the fifteenth century, the emerging "code of the samurai" required that warriors also become skilled in literature, especially in poetry, and other fine arts. This made it necessary for them to devote years of study to these new disciplines as well as keep up with the martial arts that were the core of their profession and their class.

With the coming of peace in the early decades of the Tokugawa Shogunate (1603–1868), the samurai class' involvement in the arts and crafts became even more important. Eventually it reached the point where knowledge of literature and the arts was regarded as essential to their social and moral standing.

This desire for learning became extraordinarily conspicuous in Japanese society following the fall of the shogunate government in 1868 and the rush to industrialize and modernize the economy. It is no exaggeration to say that the Japanese became obsessed with learning Western technology and Western ways.

This obsession became even stronger during the post-World War II years, when the Japanese were faced with the challenge of rebuilding their cities and their industries. Students studied until they were exhausted and often ruined their health. Japanese businessmen became famous worldwide for collecting and devouring every scrap of technological and business information they could beg, borrow, or steal.

During the 1950s and '60s hundreds of thousands of Japanese businessmen traveled abroad on research missions, visiting factories, retail outlets, and other businesses with cameras in hand and notebooks at the ready. They were samurai in everything except their apparel—and in carrying cameras instead of swords.

By the time Musashi reached the age of twenty-nine he had become undefeatable in battle, which prompted him to stop killing his opponents. He began combining his daily training in martial arts with instruction in the fine arts. He was still "in training" until the last months of his life, when illness robbed him of his strength and the use of his hands.

Musashi had the rare distinction of being relatively long lived for a samurai. He experienced and adapted to dramatic changes in the roles of the samurai in Japanese society. He had taken on all opponents, all challenges, to fulfill his lifelong goals. But in keeping with the ethics of his time, he had achieved more than becoming the greatest swordsman in the history of the country. Before the end of his life he had become a renowned calligrapher, a skilled artist, and a noted writer, known as much for his artistic accomplishments as his prowess with the sword.

This kind of successful transformation requires both continuous training and the ability to expand your goals over time. Today this kind of lifespan is taken for granted, and living longer brings with it the need to be just as adaptable and as skillful as Musashi in preserving and building on your skills and success throughout life.

CHAPTER TWENTY-THREE

Hit First; Hit Hard!

The more I read of Boye's book on the spirit of the samurai, the more convinced I became that Musashi was an embodiment of a praying mantis. Like mantids, he hit first and hit hard—a samurai concept expressed in the phrase *jigen-ryu* (jee-gane-r'yuu), a method of sword fighting based on the idea of striking first.

In this concept the first strike in a sword fight - means you win and live. If you have no choice but to try again it means your fate is sealed.

Obviously, the primary lesson in this chapter is to observe your enemy with great care, catch him off-guard and strike with lightning speed.

— *Michihiro Matsumoto*

Musashi had one unfailing rule in his encounters with opponents: Hit first and hit hard. He took this approach in all of the duels that are covered by the historical record and no doubt in all of his other duels as well. He preached this principle to his disciples, and when he set down his rules for succeeding in battle in his *Book of Five Rings*, it was one of the foundations of his way of fighting. He taught his students to:

- Strike before your opponent is ready, while he is still assuming his fighting stance.
- Catch him off guard, then strike with such power that he is shocked.
- Strike to kill, or to crush your opponent completely.

Of course, there is nothing new about this style of fighting. It was probably one of the primary tactics of primitive man tens of thousands of years ago: Get the jump on your enemy or victims and render them helpless or dead before they can protect themselves.

While Musashi was apparently the only samurai who used the "hit-first hit-hard" approach as a key part of his fighting routine, the concept was well known to the shogunate government, fief lords, and clan leaders of his time, and it was common in the civil wars and internal struggles fought throughout Japan's middle ages.

Of course, the best-known recent example of the attack-first-and-hard tactic was the Japanese aerial raid on Pearl Harbor in 1941. The offensive wars launched by the Japanese military on the Asian mainland prior to 1941 also began with all-out surprise attacks. In modern-day Japan, "the hit-first hit-hard" tactic has been integrated into everyday business strategy—with an emphasis on developing new products that are extraordinarily innovative and create large businesses quickly.

The lesson here is clear: If you find yourself in combat or competition, don't give your opponents an opportunity to settle into a strong position. Strike fast and strike hard—before they have a chance to get the upper hand.

CHAPTER TWENTY-FOUR

Use All of Your Weapons

Many great men, such as David Attenborough and Arnold Toynbee, gave religions their due, but they also followed one of Musashi's primary rules—don't depend on God to win your battles for you.

In this chapter, Boyé clearly reveals the vital importance of being well-prepared and utilizing every weapon in your arsenal when you engage an adversary in a life and death struggle.

Like Janine Benyus theorizes in her 1997 book, *Biomicry*, observing and regarding nature as a model and mentor is one of the best possible ways of coming up with solutions to problems—an approach that Musashi mastered and used from a very young age.

Most of us are not faced with life-or-death decisions on a regular basis—as Musashi was—but many of the recent so-called break-through discoveries in medicine and other fields came from observing nature in action.

Like Musashi, we can all learn valuable lessons in how to live by observing and imitating other life forms in nature; something that more and more people are coming to understand and appreciate.

— *Michihiro Matsumoto*

Musashi's motto was, "Acknowledge the gods, but don't depend on them." He, of course, depended on his own wits, abilities, and actions to succeed in combat, rather than some divine assistance.

In our society, unlimited or uninhibited conflict or competition of any kind is rare—except in "ultimate fighting" exhibitions and in terrorist acts. Academics, sports, business—even wars—are conducted according to rules of "proper behavior"—originally as determined by mutual agreement but now by public opinion polls!

In Musashi's time, however, combat and competition were driven by commonsense evaluation of goals and methods, many of which are not generally acceptable today. Musashi knew that whether or not he was successful in—or even survived—a duel depended on his using every trick, tool, and technique at his disposal. As we have seen, he would often attack opponents before they were ready. He would take advantage of the fact that fighters are vulnerable during and immediately after they attack: tricking his opponents into rushing at him and then cutting them down before they could deliver a blow.

The lesson here is obvious: In deadly conflicts use whatever tactic or technique you need to accomplish your goals. It is not enough to win the public relations battle if in the process you lose the war.

CHAPTER TWENTY-FIVE

The Samurai and the Carpenter

I have long admired one of the rules followed by the cowboys of America's West—the rule they had of first watering and feeding their horses after a long ride or hard day's work before taking care of their own needs.

Musashi taught that a samurai who wanted to avoid death should keep his weapons in good condition so that when he had to use them they would not fail him. The modern-day lesson this teaches is that we need to keep our knowledge and our skills honed to perfection if we want to survive and be the best that we can be.

If Musashi was alive today he would make an outstanding management consultant. Boyé uses the term "holistic" to describe Musashi's principle of organic management. But whatever term is used it means that every situation has a multitude of elements that must be a part of good, effective behavior (in Musashi's case, staying alive).

— *Michihiro Matsumoto*

In his lessons to his disciples, Musashi used the analogy of a carpenter. He said the samurai should think like a carpenter—in the sense of the tools a carpenter uses, how he maintains the tools, how he trains with the tools, how he plans each project, how he accounts for location and environment and all the other factors that may influence the finished product. He noted that a master carpenter must thoroughly understand the nature of the tools he uses, the materials that are the best suited for the purpose, the size and shape of the things he builds, how they are to be used, and so on.

Musashi's point was that learning how to fight and win was not a simple task with only a few elements, but incorporated a whole world of factors and possibilities that took years to master. He said that until the samurai had made himself as carefully shaped and finished as a perfect building or piece of furniture his training was incomplete and he would be vulnerable.

He made a special point of emphasizing that one of the most important skills needed by a master swordsman was insight into the nature of human beings—their strengths, their weaknesses, their spirit, and all of the different attitudes and behaviors commonly found in the makeup of people.

The point here is that individuals should continuously strive to increase their knowledge and improve themselves in a comprehensive, holistic way. Musashi

CHAPTER TWENTY-SIX

Take the Initiative

Musashi's rule of always taking the initiative in his dozens of duels to the death, even when he did not appear to his adversaries to be doing anything at all, was obviously one of the secrets of his surviving to an advanced age.

I am again reminded of the behavior of insects, reptiles, and other animals in the wild whose day-to-day survival depends upon making instant decisions that will determine whether they eat or don't eat, live or die.

Military men and corporate warriors of today need to take this lesson to heart if they are to survive and succeed in a manner and to a degree that it brings credit to them.

This includes knowing when to fight and when not to fight.

Here again, it is obvious that Musashi's incredible success in winning so many battles was based on being prepared, adapting instantly to the circumstances, and taking the initiative, either directly or indirectly.

— Michihiro Matsumoto

Another of the key principles in Musashi's tactics was to always take the initiative in every encounter—to never let your opponent determine the beginning or the progress of a fight. The obvious point to this rule is that by attacking first and seizing and keeping the advantage you can force your opponent to react to your moves rather than you having to react to his.

Musashi notes that you can maintain the initiative even when your opponent makes the first move by reacting faster than his action—taking advantage of his vulnerability during his move. He called this maneuver "stepping on the sword" of your opponent.

He did not, of course, mean literally stepping on your opponent's weapon. He meant executing a move that would counter any move your opponent made, whether it was raising his sword, lowering his sword, shifting his feet, rushing at you, or whatever. This is a secondary measure, however, since one of Musashi's primary rules in a fight is to make the first move, before your opponent has time to get ready.

As long as you are well trained and in the right frame of mind, the advantages of being the first to attack or to counter with an attack that is faster than your opponent's move are obvious in any business or competitive situation.

CHAPTER TWENTY-SEVEN

Know Your Environment

The "hidden" message in this chapter is that you are very likely to fail if you do not keep your wits about you—a condition known as *zanshin* (zahn-sheen), which may be translated as "lingering mind."

Many people—most people in fact—are not in a state of *zanshin* most of their waking hours—meaning that they are kind of coasting mentally; not focused and not being the best that they can be. They just let things slide…

Musashi obviously knew intuitively at a very young age that a fight was not over until his adversary—in blunt terms—was dead. His *zanshin* lesson is especially appropriate in today's terrorist-ridden world, but it also applies to business and all other endeavors as well.

The point is that we should be aware of what is going on around us and be prepared to take action immediately to repair or enhance any situation or relationship in which we are involved.

— *Michihiro Matsumoto*

Musashi made a point of carefully observing the environment around him for everything and anything he could take advantage of in his fights—the time of day; whether it was sunny or cloudy; whether the ground was dry, wet, uneven, rocky, or soft; the presence of rivers, lakes, trees; and so on.

In his *Book of Five Rings*, Musashi described a number of situations in which his immediate surroundings determined his tactics. Whether outside in open fields or indoors in small rooms and hallways, he emphasized the importance of knowing and using the "lay of the land" to your advantage.

While this is clearly relevant to outdoor sports competitions, its application in the business world may not be as obvious. However, any experienced executive will tell you that paying careful attention to room layout, seating arrangements, speaking order, attendees, and so forth—in other words, the geography of the meeting—is of critical importance in succeeding at business negotiations. This is especially true in Japan, where the format and routine of business meetings has been institutionalized and ritualized for centuries.

CHAPTER TWENTY-EIGHT

Watch for a Collapse

China's great military strategist Sun Tzu taught that the successful commander was one who could get inside the head of his enemy, anticipate his actions and take measures that would prevent him from carrying out his plans.

This kind of what-if thinking is common among many people, but not among the Japanese. The Japanese have never been comfortable with what-if thinking—a legacy, perhaps, of island mentality. A Japanese proverb goes: "If you think about next year, the devil will laugh at you. So don't even think 'if'."

In that respect, Musashi was more of a continental or global thinker. In any event, one of his primary strengths was in watching for—and often initiating—a break in his opponent's focus, and then cutting him down in a flash.

His mastery of managing risks (ifs) and crises (whens) resulted in him never losing a battle. This is a lesson that can be applied in virtually every area of life, from personal relationships to business and, yes, war!

— *Michihiro Matsumoto*

Musashi was keenly aware that in time all things collapse—some things over eons of time and other things
in a matter of a split second. He used the word "collapse" in reference to the conduct of an army in combat as well as the condition of an individual opponent.
He meant that the soldiers or the individual combatants lost their focus and rhythm, making them vulnerable to a swift, coordinated attack.

Musashi cautioned his disciples that they should
train themselves to the point that they could instantly
recognize when an opponent lost his rhythm and instantly spring to the attack before they could recover.
In his words, "Your rushing attack must be instanta-
neous and strong, and you must cut him down with
such vigor that he cannot recover." He further warned
his disciples that they should thoroughly understand
what he meant by "cutting down with vigor."

This advice is, of course, applicable in business,
politics, sports, and war.

CHAPTER TWENTY-NINE

Become Your Opponent

This is another lesson that is just common sense, but it is so simple that many people gloss over it. What Musashi did not say in this lesson is that he spent more time studying the tactics of other warriors than he did practicing swordsmanship.

As a result of his intense study of how people behave when faced with any kind of challenge, he became so adept at anticipating the behavior of his opponents that he could virtually read their minds. In fact, for all practical purposes, that is precisely what he did.

A not-so-obvious lesson to be learned from Musashi's instructions to his disciples is that to master a skill that can mean the difference between life and death it must be taken very seriously. He himself was so serious in his training and in his behavior in general that many of his compatriots considered him abnormal.

— *Michihiro Matsumoto*

The ancient Chinese military sage Sun Tzu taught that one of the primary principles of victory in war was to know your enemy. Musashi's version of this precept was to figuratively "become your opponent"—to get "inside" your opponent's head to the point that you could think like him and thus anticipate any move he might make and strike first.

Musashi described the warrior who could think "only in his own head" as a pheasant holed up in a house, while the man who was going to cut him down was described as a hawk. Musashi said that if you demonstrate the ability to "read your opponent's mind" he will be so intimidated that he will become fearful, make mistakes, and give you an opportunity to defeat him.

He added that if you cannot "see inside of your opponent's head" you should pretend that you do and make a move indicating that you are going to launch an immediate attack. This results in your opponent showing his hand, allowing you to instantly change the nature of your attack, and catch him unprepared. He refers to this ploy as "moving the shadow."

This lesson, too, is applicable in any competitive situation, and particularly so in sports, business, and war.

CHAPTER THIRTY

Draw Your Opponent In

Faking your opponents out is a ruse that is well known in all cultures, and thus appears to be an instinct that we are born with. One of Sun Tzu's most insightful and memorable rules was keep your friends close and your enemies closer—something, however, that many present-day politicians and statesmen seem to have forgotten.

In Japan we have a number of traditional rituals that are based on this theme, including *Setsubun* (sate-sue-boon), the bean-throwing ceremony that involves a polite, friendly way of inviting evil spirits to leave your home. This, of course, is an emotional approach to handling such matters.

It has also been common in history for people to entice those they perceive as enemies into their web and then destroy them. Musashi became a master at enticing his adversaries into his net, providing a valuable lesson to those facing threats from the outside.

Of course, in this day and age it is advisable to make use of another lesson taught by Musashi—how to win battles by not fighting...by being so strong that no one will challenge you.

— *Michihiro Matsumoto*

One of the most common tactics Musashi used to give himself an advantage over his opponents was to behave in a casual or lackadaisical manner, resulting in the opponent becoming less watchful and more careless— a move he called "drawing your opponent in." This tactic is, of course, well known, especially to boxers, who employ it to mount swift attacks on their opponents, scoring points and sometimes ending contests with one or two blows.

In a somewhat humorous note, Musashi likened this strategy to getting your opponents drunk. He also related this tactic to acting so unthreatening that your opponent becomes bored, lowers his defenses, and is more susceptible to being crushed by a light-ning strike.

The tactic of "drawing an opponent in" has long been an integral part of Japanese culture—not in the manner suggested by Musashi, but as a result of a built-in "humble mode" that historically has resulted in adversaries and competitors underestimating the abilities, strength, and spirit of the Japanese. The samurai culture that endured from the twelfth to the nineteenth century in Japan made it mandatory that common people—and the samurai themselves when interacting with their own superiors—behave in a humble way to avoid giving offense and to maintain a façade of harmony.

This cultural behavior is still very much alive in contemporary Japan and continues to give the Japanese a special advantage in their dealings with others. A significant part of this advantage is the reaction of typical Westerners when they encounter people who are less experienced, less skilled than they are. These Westerners, Americans in particular, instantly go into a "help mode" and go out of their way to help those they perceive as less capable.

The Japanese have long been aware of the "help syndrome" that drives Westerners, and they naturally take advantage of it. In any event, it goes without saying that humility will get you much further than arrogance and braggadocio, and this is something that Musashi thoroughly understood and used with extraordinary success.

CHAPTER THIRTY-ONE

Never Use the Same Tactic Twice

The lesson in this chapter is that continuous creativity is often the essential ingredient in any kind of success—whether in business, politics or social situations. But people in all categories of life are prone to getting hung up on using the same tactics in an effort to achieve the same old strategic goals.

This is a weakness that eventually leads to some degree of failure whatever the goals might be...and is something that Musashi took to heart. His inventiveness was often so commonplace, so simple, that his opponents were thrown completely off-guard and were easily defeated.

In my jargon, strategy should be as solid as a rock, while tactics should be as flexible as the wind. I follow the example of Musashi, flexibly changing my tactics but without deviating from my strategic goals.

I never make the same speech twice, but I*never deviate from *Bushidō* or *Eigodō*. The *Dō* or "The Way" is embedded in my soul as my moral compass. That's strategy. And I will follow it for as long as I live—as Musashi did.

— *Michihiro Matsumoto*

Another of Musashi's rules of combat was never to use the same tactic more than twice—and never more than once if you could help it. His obvious intent was to prevent any of his opponents from becoming familiar enough with his style of fighting that they could prepare themselves to counter it.

Conventional wisdom encourages us to develop, or "engineer," specific methods or processes for doing things—and then repeat them over and over again. This is especially true in situations involving teams and groups and is even more of a factor in large organizations such as corporations, government ministries, and armies. The rationale, of course, is that to achieve shared goals, groups must work in unison in a consistent way. Musashi, of course, would not have agreed. He would have pointed out the danger in consistent and predictable behavior—whether in a duel to the death or competing in tough world markets.

In the past, Japanese culture was the epitome of the organized, prescribed way of doing things. But this started to change during the 1990s as the famous "bubble economy" began to deflate. In desperate efforts to revitalize the economy, Japanese companies turned their most innovative employees loose, letting them work outside of the highly structured company system. They not only separated them from the hierarchical corporate structures, they arranged for separate financing.

The results were extraordinary. Virtually all of the new "side enterprises" flourished, with many of them playing major roles in returning their parent companies to profitability.

This lesson has not been lost on the Japanese, and it is an invaluable lesson for people, companies, and organizations everywhere. You must learn to adapt and change if you want to survive. If you want to be a winner, like Musashi, you must constantly develop new ways of competing, new techniques for overcoming the challenges you face.

CHAPTER THIRTY-TWO

Make Your Opponent Change His Style of Fighting

There is always a certain rhythm to the planning of combat, negotiations, and other human interactions—a rhythm that is always susceptible to being upset and resulting in what the military people like to call "the fog of war."

The lesson in this chapter is that you can invariably confuse and weaken an adversary by forcing him to change his style or way of negotiating or fighting. As pointed out in earlier chapters, people get so hung up on specific forms that they are incapable of changing quickly—or at all in many cases.

The very first thing that martial artists must do is grasp the form and rhythm of their opponents and quickly construct tactics to overcome them. You might call this the strategy of manipulating your opponents' rhythm. Boyé calls it making your opponent change his style of fighting.

Musashi himself went much further in his teachings, explaining it in esoteric terms of universal spatial relationships. However you want to define it, it is a tactic that works.

— *Michihiro Matsumoto*

Another secret of Musashi's incredible success in armed combat was his ability to force his opponents to change their style of fighting. Musashi could read the slightest movement of an opponent's sword, feet, eyes, or hands; recognize their intentions; and adjust his fighting style accordingly. His broad knowledge of the martial arts and his ability to switch to a more effective style at will gave him an unbeatable advantage.

If his opponents couldn't react and adapt their own fighting approach—especially if they knew only one style of fighting—he would launch an attack against which they had no defense. In most cases his fights were over in seconds. If, on the other hand, an opponent was experienced enough to shift to another style, Musashi would keep the advantage by forcing them to change again and again until they tried a technique they weren't so good at. Then he would cut them down in a flash.

Musashi's experience, adaptability, and reputation gave him an important psychological advantage over his opponents. They knew that even if they could come up with an effective defense for one of his styles of fighting, Musashi would just switch to another style.

Again, this is a testament to the tactical values of unpre- dictability, the importance of broad knowledge of fighting techniques, the willingness to take the initiative in competition, and the cleverness to stay one step ahead of your opponents. In terms of contemporary competition, it also speaks to the need for broad tactical flexibility and the willingness to change the terms of the competition.

CHAPTER THIRTY-THREE

Behave As If You Were Already Dead

This is an easy lesson to grasp, but it is very difficult for people in life-is-sacred cultures to adopt and use. Musashi said repeatedly in his treatise that a great deal of his amazing success in meeting and killing so many opponents was that he did not think about being killed or behaving in a cautious manner to protect his own life.

He said that in all of his death-duel encounters he always took the position that he was already dead and therefore had no reason to fear being cut down by his opponent.

This attitude can be attributed to sheer foolhardy recklessness or to absolute conviction in the superiority of one's skills and tactics. In Musashi's case, the latter was apparently true. His confidence in his ability was surely unbounded.

Still today in Kagoshima on the southern tip of Kyushu Island (one of the last strongholds of the samurai near the end of the 19th century), it is still common to hear people say, *keshin kagi kibare* (kay-sheen kah-

ghee kee-bah-ray), meaning "behave as if you were already dead"—a famous military slogan of that area
since ancient times.

It was a small group of samurai from this area who
regarded themselves as already dead that brought the
downfall of the weakened and ineffective Shogunate
government in Edo (Tokyo) when Japan was threatened
by Western countries in the 1850s and 1860s.

Nowadays, this kind of behavior in war (and in normal
life) still occurs, but it is almost always an action that is
not planned, happening on the spur of the moment when
facing some crises. And if such actions are witnessed by
the right people, the individuals involved are often cele-
brated as heroes whether or not they survive.

— *Michihiro Matsumoto*

As noted by Inazo Nitobe in *Bushido: The Soul of Japan*,
the bedrock of the samurai code was personal honor.
To a samurai, the fear of being shamed, of being disgraced, was greater than the love of life. Often, a simple slip in upholding one's honor or the honor of one's
family could be resolved only by suicide.

One of the primary principles of the education of a
samurai was for them to achieve the state of mind in
which they regarded themselves as already dead—a
mind-set that left them with no fears for their life, no
second-guessing of their abilities, and no reason for
avoiding life-threatening situations.

Musashi had apparently already absorbed this lesson by the time he was thirteen, when he challenged and killed a veteran swordsman—or he had such incredible confidence in his ability at that young age that he was absolutely certain that he would win and was therefore fearless. Later in life Musashi instructed his own disciples in the principle of behaving as if they were already dead, so it can surely be assumed that this mind-set also played a vitally important role in his own survival and success.

According to Yamamoto Tsunetomo (in *Hagakure: The Book of the Samurai*, translated by William Scott Wilson), "When on the battlefield, if you try not to let others take the lead and have the solid intention of breaking into the enemy lines, then you will not fall behind others. Your mind will become fierce, and you will manifest martial valor. Furthermore, if you are slain in battle, you should resolve to have your corpse facing the enemy."

The lesson to be learned from this samurai code is that one must be prepared to go all the way in achieving great goals. The modern-day equivalent of this attitude is demonstrated in many ways in business, fighting, gambling, and in sports, when individuals and groups take high risks in pursuit of goals.

CHAPTER THIRTY-FOUR

Avoid Stalemates

Smart military commanders, politicians and statesmen are aware that getting stuck in a rut is often a harbinger of failure. Musashi was acutely aware of this danger and always went to extremes to avoid getting involved in a stalemate in his battles.

Alas! Modern Japan has produced millions of disarmed and de-spiritualized samurai businesspeople who have not succeeded because they have accepted a stalemate of one kind or another.

Stalemates kill innovation—and innovation was one of the most valuable traits in Musashi's arsenal of weapons.

Fortunately, there is still enough of the samurai spirit in Japan that the stalemate mentality that afflicted the Japanese in the 1990s has begun to dissipate, and the economy and society in general is once again on the upswing.

The lesson, here, of course, is: never allow yourself to be stalemated in a game, in business, or in war.

— *Michihiro Matsumoto*

Musashi emphasized the importance of avoiding stale-mates at all costs, regarding them as failures. He noted that stalemates occur most often when people attempt impractical ventures that they should have avoided in the first place. The worst such stalemates happen during wars, as has been graphically and horribly demonstrated throughout history—from the Trojan War to Korea and Vietnam.

Musashi's approach to combat—constantly changing his style or forcing his opponents to change theirs, confusing and rattling his opponents, and so on—was also designed to avoid stalemates and win. Nevertheless, a few of his demonstration or "comparison of technique" fights ended in draws—with neither side able to gain an advantage. It is probably safe to assume, however, that given Musashi's track record he would have found a way to achieve a decisive victory if the fights had been to the death.

The lesson here is obvious. You should always prepare backup plans that you can turn to quickly if you're faced with a stalemate. In fact, you should have a number of backup plans ready so that you can break any kind of deadlock. Even the smallest advantage generated by changing your approach or introducing some other element can break a stalemate and make a complete victory possible.

CHAPTER THIRTY-FIVE

Never Give
Your Opponent
a Second Chance

One of the principles by which Musashi lived—literally as well as figuratively—was never turning the other cheek to an opponent after having achieved an advantage over him. In virtually all of his battles if his first blow did not kill his opponent he made absolutely sure the second one did.

This may sound cruel and inhuman to some people raised in Christian societies, but Musashi believed in and followed the second side in the two-sided concept of *kejime* (kay-jee-may), which refers to a line that should not be crossed or a line that should be crossed. He chose to cross the line by making sure that his opponents were dead and would therefore never again pose a threat.

Where one draws a line is determined by one's culture and the occasion. In most societies married men and women are not supposed to flirt to the extent of "crossing the line" out of consideration for *kejime*—the discernment between right and wrong.

However, making victory complete and final is considered mandatory for consummating any contract or
commitment, emotional, aesthetic, ethical, logical, or
legal, thereby fulfilling the dictates of *kejime*.

The point here is to be insightful enough to know
when and where to draw a line and not cross over it.

— *Michihiro Matsumoto*

Another of Musashi's rules was to make sure that his
opponents couldn't make a comeback. At least in his
earlier years, he didn't believe in defeating or incapaci-
tating his opponents and then withdrawing from the
battle. His policy was to kill them.

Musashi believed that you should take the initiative
in everything at all times, never letting your opponent
rest or regroup—literally never letting an opponent
have time to think. He was also adamant about taking
advantage of an enemy at the first sign of what he
called their "collapse"—meaning any sign of uncoordi-
nated behavior.

This, he said, provided an opening to rush in with
great force and crush the opponent. This may seem
savage, but it was the reality of Musashi's times. There
is also a lesson here that applies to modern-day combat
and competition: Don't stop short of neutralizing your
opponent's ability to retaliate.

Most people avoid conflict—at work, in competition, or at home. There is a natural tendency to with-

draw, compromise, or relent. The lesson we can learn from Musashi is that when the stakes are high (in his case, life or death) you cannot afford to give your opponent an opportunity to recover and possibly turn defeat into victory or simply prolong the fighting and make the outcome uncertain. His message: Don't stop until your victory is complete, total and final.

This lesson was typically applied on a national scale throughout Japan's early history. One famous example: In 1588 Hideyoshi Toyotomi, a reigning warlord during Japan's shogunate era, issued an edict that required all non-samurai to turn in all swords, spears, guns, and any other weapons they had to local officials. The edict made it a major offense for anyone other than the ruling samurai class to have weapons.

As planned, Hideyoshi's edict made it impossible for the common people of Japan to take any kind of mass military action against the samurai class and the government. His policy, continued by his successors, eventually led to several generations of peace for the Japanese and dramatically reduced the incidence of murder and other crimes of violence—helping to make Japan one of the safest societies on earth.

CHAPTER THIRTY-SIX

Pierce the Bottom

There were rare occasions when Musashi did not kill his adversaries for one reason or another, but on these occasions he made sure that he did something that was even more devastating to his adversaries—he killed their spirits.

Musashi knew from history and from the events of his own time that if you left enemies wounded but still desirous of victory and revenge they were even more dangerous than before. He therefore made certain that any opponent he left alive was so dispirited that he would never pose any kind of threat to him.

This is a lesson that still rings true today—especially in the battles with terrorists whose ideology propels them to destroy themselves and innocents in order to kill their enemies.

If the spirit of the samurai should return to Japan full blown there would surely be another revolution, and Japan would be transformed from a materially rich country to a spiritually rich country. It is better to be

poor and honest and environmentally friendly than to be
dishonest and rich.

If Japan's traditional spirit is completely destroyed,
that will be the end of the line for Japan, so as Boyé
says, samurai-type education should be restored.

— *Michihiro Matsumoto*

Musashi repeated himself endlessly in his efforts to
help his disciples become master swordsmen. He called one of his key lessons "piercing the bottom"—a
euphemistic way of referring to the spirit of adversaries, and something he emphasized in different ways
in virtually all of his instructions.

In Musashi's view there were two facets to victory.
First, the opponent or opponents should be killed as
quickly and as expeditiously as possible. And second,
if any opponents were left alive, their spirit should be
totally destroyed so that they would never again present a threat.

Musashi called the destruction of the spirit of an
enemy "piercing the bottom"—meaning that the mind
of the opponent is "pierced" as if with a spear or sword
and therefore is "dead." He warned again and again
that you should not stop your attack just because your
enemy slacks off and/or retreats, because this does not
mean that their "bottom has been pierced"—that there
is no more hostility, no more ambition, in their hearts.

He instructed his disciples to redouble their efforts when an enemy appeared to be losing, quickly "adjusting" their own minds to continue the attack until they were absolutely certain that the spirit of the enemy had been crushed.

This harsh-sounding advice may not be considered appropriate for most nonviolent situations today, but its power cannot be denied.

CHAPTER THIRTY-SEVEN

The Importance
of Art in Life

Despite a lifelong rigorous regime of training his mind and body to kill or defeat opponents in one-on-one sword fights, Musashi was also the product of a culture that regarded art as essential for the fulfillment of human aspirations, and in the last half of his life he became an artist as well as a warrior.

One of the most important elements in the mindset of Musashi was the existence of a view or belief in the Buddhist concept of *mushin* (moo-sheen), meaning "no mind"—a state of mind that refers to acting without artifices, without illusions, without being influenced by subjective thinking.

This is the same approach to life followed by the famed Indian philosopher J. Krishnamurti, who argued that organized religions and philosophies are obstacles to truth. Bruce Lee, one of the greatest martial artists of all time, also had a *mushin* view of the world and himself. He said that he had no style but that he was *all style*!

Everything that Musashi did was done with the eye and the heart of the consummate artist. He turned *Bushidō* into poetry in motion, providing a lesson for all who are desirous of mastering any skill.

— *Michihiro Matsumoto*

Musashi was in his late twenties before he realized that being the greatest swordsman in the land was not enough—that in order to be fulfilled as a human being it was essential that he become skilled in other areas as well. He then took up the study of several of the arts and crafts of the day, approaching each of them with the same focus and dedication that had made him master of the sword. Within a few years he was acclaimed for his poetry, drawings, sculptures, and pottery, and thereafter he took more pride in these accomplishments than in his ability with a sword.

The importance of art in human life is taken for granted today, but it is too often forgotten after one finishes elementary school. Thereafter its practice plays little or no role in the life of the average person.

Another lesson that can be learned from Musashi is that training and practicing in a number of arts should continue throughout one's life. One of Musashi's most repeated instructions to his disciples was: "Touch upon all of the arts. Develop a discerning eye in all matters." This idea is still reflected today in Japanese culture.

CHAPTER THRITY-EIGHT

The Sword of the Spirit

It has been proven repeatedly throughout history that the success or failure of individuals as well as societies is determined by the strength and quality of the spirit of the people concerned. For reasons that are not historically clear, Musashi was endowed with an incredible spirit that made him one of a kind.

The late Sen Nishiyama, the American-born Japanese-American who became the official interpreter for the American Embassy in Tokyo in the 1950s, and was my mentor when I also worked for the embassy as a simultaneous interpreter, was such a man.

In addition to teaching me that the being an interpreter required extraordinary *kihaku* (kee-hah-koo), fighting spirit or killer instinct, he was instrumental in getting interpreters treated as skilled human beings instead of faceless machines.

The lesson here, obviously, is for you to cultivate a true spirit not be bounded or restrained by ancient forms and myths—to be a samurai with a fighting spirit at all times, on stage and off-stage.

— *Michihiro Matsumoto*

Physical skills and knowledge may be worthless if you don't have a strong spirit—in the sense of courage, determination, will power, and vigor. This may not seem like an original concept, but it is a vital one when the stakes are high and you could lose your life or everything you have dreamed about and worked for in an instant.

It was Musashi's belief that a strong spirit was as important as the weapon you used in fighting. He referred to his approach as "the sword of the spirit," meaning that when wielded properly, spirit could be as formidable as a cutting blade. (In the early years of World War II the Japanese believed that their samurai spirit would make it possible for them to defeat the much larger and more powerful United States.)

Musashi's extraordinary spirit was, in fact, one of his most important weapons. Without an indomitable spirit, it's unlikely he would have rushed in to attack a seasoned warrior—known and feared as a master swordsman—in his first duel. He demonstrated the same spirit in all of his hundreds of encounters with opponents throughout his relatively long life. He was still intimidating powerful warriors half his age when he was in his fifties.

Military commanders, corporate executives, and competitors at all levels should obviously cultivate their own fighting spirit. They should also make a great effort to build and sustain the spirits of the men and women who make up their organizations. People who do not understand and promote the importance of spirit should not be in charge of anybody.

It goes without saying that a small number of fighters or workers who are endowed with an indomitable spirit can achieve extraordinary success against much larger forces. In Musashi's words, one such man can defeat ten men; ten such men can beat one hundred, and so on into the thousands. This advice is extremely—and obviously—relevant if you are part of a small company or organization facing much larger competitors. A strong spirit is absolutely essential if you are going to succeed.

CHAPTER THIRTY-NINE

Focus on Winning

As everybody knows, there are people with winning attitudes and people with losing attitudes, and it doesn't take a rocket scientist to pick those who are the most likely to succeed in life.

One of the most important lessons that Musashi taught his disciples was to develop, hone, and sustain a winning attitude. He knew only too well that unless a samurai had a winning attitude he was not likely to survive his first fight.

Some people are born with a winning attitude; others have to develop it one way or the other. Wise advice from a mentor can mean the difference between success and failure. Deliberately exposing one's self to challenges, particularly in rigorous martial arts, can also be a major factor in developing a winning attitude.

And remarkably, as far as Japan's future is concerned, more foreigners than Japanese now practice martial arts. If the trend for the Japanese to ignore the benefits of martial arts training is not reversed, I fear for the future—Musashi is probably spinning in his grave!

Sports that have not yet been transformed into entertainment are also a path to developing a winning attitude. Whatever you choose, it should be with a samurai-like commitment.

— *Michihiro Matsumoto*

One of the most important elements in Musashi's philosophy was what he called a "winning attitude." By this he meant that the mind should be totally focused on winning when one was engaged in battle.

In his own battles he made every effort possible to rid his mind of fears, doubts, or reservations of any kind that might distract him. Every fiber of his being, both his mind and his body, was focused on one goal: to win quickly and absolutely.

He stressed that warriors should not neglect their weapons or go into battle expecting to die. In his words, a warrior should always go into combat prepared for—and expecting—victory. And yet, he noted that there were occasions when forfeiting one's life in a hopeless battle was the right thing to do.

This focus on victory at all costs is captured by Yamamoto Tsunetomo in *Hagakure*: "No matter if the enemy has thousands of men, there is fulfillment in simply standing them off and being determined to cut them down, starting from one end. You will finish the greater part of it."

The ability to single-mindedly focus on winning is, of course, a common trait of great champions in sports and other endeavors. But it usually does not apply to people going about their day-to-day affairs—they have not disciplined their minds or bodies to that degree.

We could all benefit from some samurai-like training in perseverance, purpose, and this kind of positive thinking.

CHAPTER FORTY

The Head of a Rat, the Neck of a Bull

Musashi was obviously one of the most cunning and courageous men who ever lived and his life is an example of how far these traits can take one. Of course, I am not advocating that anyone pursue these traits for the same reasons that Musashi did, but in combination with other traits of the samurai they can greatly increase your chances of succeeding in living a good life.

These additional traits include *hinkaku* (heen-kah-koo), dignity, and *kigai* (kee-guy), spirit. I liken dignity to granite and spirit to fiery magma...and it is the power of spirit that supports dignity.

— *Michihiro Matsumoto*

One of the core concepts of the samurai code, which was passed on to Japan's modern military forces as well as the Japanese in general, was that in any kind of competition when you do not seem to be making progress you should keep foremost in your thoughts "the head of a rat and the neck of a bull." This saying is a reference to the cleverness of the rat and the courage, stamina, and the persistence of a bull.

Musashi's manual on his way of fighting emphasized the importance of this concept in individual duels, in military combat on any scale, and in any challenge or task undertaken by ordinary people. Here again, we see that the foundation of Musashi's approach to fighting and winning was based on common sense raised to a high level. Despite couching the details of his strategy and tactics in esoteric and philosophical terms, they were, in fact, pragmatic and practical to the core.

And just as obviously, the cleverness of the rat and the courage and persistence of the bull are characteristics that everyone should seek to develop.

CHAPTER FORTY-ONE

Surpass Today What You Were Yesterday

One of the basic principles of the training of samurai, particularly in the case of Musashi, was the concept of endeavoring to make yourself better today than you were yesterday, and to repeat this challenge on a daily basis.

This, too, is part of the *kaizen* or continuous improvement mentality that has been a basic part of Japanese culture from ancient times—a trait that can be traced to the *Shintō* spirit of the "eternal now." In case you do not know, *Shintō* is not a religious dogma; it is a natural way of life.

Despite the profession that Musashi followed from the age of thirteen until he was in his late twenties—enhancing his skills as a swordsman by fighting other samurai to the death—he obeyed the laws of nature, and during the last half of his life he became an extraordinary model of human achievement (he stopped killing is opponents when he was in his late twenties).

The *kaizen* element in Japanese culture is not what was called "constructive destruction" by economist and political scientist Joseph A. Schumpeter. It is "continuous improvement," and when I retire, like Musashi and other samurai leaders, I expect to retire into eternal self-improvement.

— *Michihiro Matsumoto*

The one core message in all of the teaching of Musashi for achieving mastery in swordsmanship and other endeavors is that your focus and dedication must be ongoing and never wane. He expressed this principle by saying "you must surpass today what you were yesterday."

This concept is another of Musashi's lessons that became an integral part of Japanese culture, permeating it from top to bottom. The saying is still commonly used by writers, speakers, instructors, and teachers. And it is at the heart of the Japanese concept expressed in the now well-known word kaizen (kigh-zen), which translates as "continuous improvement."

There is a tendency in other cultures for most people to stop training, to stop trying to improve, after they reach a certain level of skill—and this is one of the reasons why the Japanese have had an advantage in virtually everything they do. They have been culturally conditioned to never stop training.

It goes without saying that introducing the concept of striving each day to surpass the you of yesterday into education systems around the world could have a remarkable effect in helping to raise the skill levels of people in general. This phenomenon would in turn contribute across the board to the quality of life. People in all areas of life should take this lesson to heart.

CHAPTER FORTY-TWO

Perseverance and Diligence

There is, perhaps, no more telling testimony to the diligence and perseverance of Musashi than his daily efforts to surpass what he was the day before in his understanding of human nature, his ability to see and understand the environment around him, and to mobilize these attributes in a single instant of action.

Many of Japan's greatest samurai, including contemporary novelist, playwright, and consummate samurai Yukio Mishima, understood and commented on this view of life and the world.

The lesson in this chapter is, of course, the importance of diligence and perseverance in the pursuit of life. When these attributes are combined with a well-founded spirit of self-sacrifice we have the best of all worlds.

— *Michihiro Matsumoto*

It's obvious that to succeed in any difficult and serious undertaking one must persevere—that is, persist in and remain constant to a purpose, an idea, or a task in the face of obstacles and disappointments. And yet, the value and benefits accruing from perseverance are not deeply ingrained in the minds of many people.

The concept of perseverance was one of the foundations of the samurai culture and was epitomized by the mind-set and behavior of Musashi. He established a goal and never wavered in his pursuit of it. This trait, a part of the training of all samurai, became characteristic of all Japanese as the generations passed—and it is one of the main contributing factors in what the Japanese have achieved since 1945. Perseverance remains a key element in the acculturation of the Japanese and is still conspicuously visible in the character of the majority.

Another trait that has distinguished the Japanese for generations is diligence in every thing they do—diligence that made them capable of achieving extraordinary things; particularly in business and in war. Between 1870 and 1890, the Japanese transformed their country from a handicraft and agricultural base into a fully industrialized economy. Between 1945 and 1970, they not only rebuilt Japan following the devastation of World War II, they turned the country into the world's second largest economy.

CONCLUSION

The Renewal of the Samurai Spirit

Until the last decades of the twentieth century, virtually all Japanese were trained with samurai-like intensity in their work, in their sports, and in their cultural pursuits—the results of which have been dramatically demonstrated to the world. Modern-day Japanese culture has been diluted to the point that this kind of training in childhood and during the teen years is no longer typical. What the effects of this will be in the future are unclear, but they surely will not be positive.

However, the samurai spirit gained a new lease on life as a result of the collapse of Japan's so-called "economic bubble" in the early 1990s. The shock was felt throughout the country, resulting in corporate leaders, educators, and government leaders calling on a return to the samurai-like discipline and diligence that had once been taken for granted.

All of these calls for a renewal of the samurai spirit, combined with the reality of the shame and disappointment felt by the Japanese, resulted in a boom in the sales of books on the samurai code, and the proliferation of *dojo* teaching *Kendo* (Ken-doh), "The Way of the Sword." If this "transfusion" of the samurai spirit continues long enough, it will help keep Japan a major player in the global economy.

Of course all people everywhere are aware of the benefits of intensive training, but there are still lessons to be learned from the samurai approach of beginning such training in early childhood and continuing it throughout life.

—*OWARI*—